I0623393

I AM NOT YOUR
BRUH

I AM NOT YOUR
BRUH

21 Keys to Sound Parenting

George Mekhail

Foreword by Peter McCormack

Bitcoin Magazine Books
Nashville, TN

I Am Not Your Bruh by George Mekhail

© 2024 by George Mekhail; No portion of this book may be reproduced, distributed, or transmitted in whole or part without written permission of the publishers. Please maintain author and publisher information, including this page and metadata, with any reproduction, distribution, or transmission, in whole or in part.

ISBN 979-8-9891326-9-0 (Paperback)
ISBN 979-8-9857289-4-1 (eBook)

BITCOIN MAGAZINE BOOKS

Published by Bitcoin Magazine Books
An imprint of BTC Media, LLC
300 10th Avenue South, Nashville, TN 37203

Address all queries to contact@btcmedia.org

Cover design by Saxyn Mekhail

Editorial advisor Danielle Mekhail

Interior design by MediaNeighbours.com

The views and conclusions expressed in this manuscript are entirely the author's own and do not necessarily reflect those of BTC Media, LLC or its employees, agents, partners, and associates.

Bitcoin Magazine Books is a trademark of BTC Media, LLC, all rights reserved, and may not be reproduced without written permission of the publisher.

For Danielle, Kingston, and Saxyn aka FamBam

CONTENTS

FOREWORD

By Peter McCormack

Being asked to write a foreword for a book is always an honour, but when George hit me up and said, "Mate, I'm writing a book on parenting," my first thought was, "Why the hell are you asking me?" I mean, sure, I've got a couple of kids, but I've messed up plenty as a dad. What advice could I give?

I was thrown into the deep end of fatherhood in a totally unplanned fashion at the tender age of 25. As I now reflect on my journey as a parent, my greatest shortfall was perhaps the mismanagement of time. Driven by career ambitions, my children made many sacrifices, as I missed out on countless irreplaceable moments, from school events to family dinners. As I worked tirelessly, I told them the old cliche of trying to give them the best life I could provide, but the truth is the life they really wanted was one with their Dad. They don't know or understand the financial pressures of the modern world. All they know is Dad is too busy again.

This echoes my own childhood, where my dad was always busy working, tired, and stressed. Yet he has been a fantastic granddad, dedicating his retirement years to the grandchildren he adores. The idea of becoming a granddad myself is now a more likely event than having more children. If you had asked me five years ago about having grandchildren, I would have freaked out, saying I'm not that old. But ask me now and I am excited by the idea, because like my dad I have time.

As I find myself closer to retirement than the start of my career, I am consciously aware of time. The adage that "an inch of time is worth an inch of gold, but you can't buy an inch of time with an inch of gold" comes to mind. I think about this a lot. My son will soon turn 20 and is in Africa, building his adult life, and in four short years my daughter will head to university. Realising that their childhood years are nearly behind me is both sobering and a catalyst for introspection. Money has given me time, but I can't buy back the time I have lost as a parent.

The relentless pace of modern life, compounded by economic pressures, demands more of our time than ever before. The era when a single income could sustain a household, allowing one parent to devote themselves fully to child-rearing, seems like a distant memory. The pervasive threat of inflation only exacerbates this challenge, eroding the very fabric of family time and well-being. In this context, I've come to appreciate the value of Bitcoin as a means to reclaim time. By safeguarding our financial resources against the crime of inflation, Bitcoin offers a semblance of freedom, enabling us to prioritise what truly matters.

The scarcity of time, much like the finite nature of Bitcoin, is a reality that demands our attention and respect. Bitcoin has given me time to reclaim some of those childhood years;

but as a legacy I leave for my kids, I hope it gives them the freedom to save time for their children and my future grandchildren.

As you delve into George's book, please do not consider it a guide to becoming the perfect parent. You will figure out how to be a parent yourself and make your own mistakes. Instead, see George's book as tips from someone who has figured parenting out better than most. Having spent time with his son Kingston, I can vouch for the remarkably respectful, intelligent, and engaging young man he is raising. He speaks volumes about George's approach to fatherhood.

While I wish I had the insights from George's book during my early days as a parent, I am grateful for the lessons I learned reading it now. Kids don't need much more than love and time; if you can give them both, you are more than halfway there.

INTRODUCTION

I t's an exciting, terrifying, and momentous time to be alive. There is almost too *much* change in the air. The pace at which the world is being transformed before our eyes presents a daunting and at times depressing outlook for parents. With change comes uncertainty, and with uncertainty comes fear, and with fear we can quickly begin to lose hope. While I wish I had all the answers for how to navigate this chaos, I'm afraid it's not that simple. If you're a parent, looking to resolve the tension of an ever-changing world for your kids, you're going to be disappointed in what follows. This book encourages you to admit the world is hard right now. Learning to embrace this simple truth will allow you to rise to the occasion and begin to anticipate the dynamics of our evolving landscape while more effectively confronting every new challenge. Despite the challenges we face as we find ourselves raising children in this brave new world, there is also an abundance of opportunity if we are willing to seek it out. We have a duty to pursue hope for the sake of the next generation—we've got kids to raise after all!

Parenting is hard work. Sound parenting, the philosophy we explore in this book, is even harder. Throughout these pages you'll find practical tools which, if implemented, can make a significant impact on your children. These are not abstract theories or unqualified opinions. This is what my wife Danielle and I have been practicing and the foundation we've built our entire parenting strategy around for the past 16 years. As you dive into these recommendations, I want to acknowledge that everyone's experience is dynamic. Not all kids are the same and there is only so much nuance that can be packed into a single book. At the end of the day, you must exercise your best judgment as you attempt to experiment with these suggestions. Your unique situation and active discernment is required with each tactic you decide to try in your own home. I also want to encourage you to challenge these ideas against competing parental strategies and question the logic behind the advice throughout this book. We certainly did! You are not going to read one book and have it all figured out. That said, if this *is* the only book you pore over, I want to ensure you handle each word you read with the same level of care I have attempted to put into these pages, if only because parenting is not for the faint of heart.

Seriously, I Am Not Your Bruh

You've got kids. You are the parent; they are the child. Here's an unpopular opinion: No one else will come close to being the mom or dad your children truly need. Yes, they may have uncles, aunts, grandparents, and other influential people in their lives. These people may be family, friends, teachers, or coaches. They may even leave valuable impressions on them throughout their upbringing. That's fantastic! There is deep truth in the saying, "It takes a village." But none of these people can or will ever replace the essential role of their mother and father.

Parents who prioritize being overly chummy with their kids have a fundamental misunderstanding of the critical and irreplaceable role they play in the lives of their offspring. While it may be well intended or even innocent, it is in fact selfish, immature, and short-sighted. Often these are the parents who want to retain their youth or revive their glory days by living vicariously through their kids. This results in sad attempts to appear "cool" to their kids and sometimes even their kids' friends. Yikes. Please stop. You are a walking "how do you do fellow kids" meme.

"I am not your friend, I am your father [or mother]." Say it again! Vocabulary is one of the most essential tools in the parental tool belt. The power of language can't be overstated. This means that one of the basics of Sound Parenting is ensuring your children refer to you as "Mom" or "Dad" or "Papa" or "Mommy" or whatever language clearly expresses the nature of the relationship. One time my son Kingston called me "George." That's the end of that story because it only happened once. I am not "yo," I am not "dude," I am not "hey man," I'm "Dad." I love you more than I can explain. I love you *too* much to *only* be your friend. Please let me know if you have any questions.

PARENTS: BIG HUMANS RESPONSIBLE FOR LITTLE HUMANS

You are your kid's hero, even if you kinda suck sometimes. They worship you. Actually, even if you completely suck most of the time, they still want to be *just like you*. This is meant to be a bit of a terrifying thought which hopefully helps motivate you to suck a little less. For the kids. When I fall short of my own expectations as a father—say I lose my cool and raise my voice or something—there is no worse feeling in the world. And that's good, because it's my conscience reminding me to check myself.

Being granted the sacred honor of having children is one of life's most precious gifts. This is why it is unacceptable to become a parent and then abdicate that honor in exchange for wanting to be or acting as if you were merely a friend. This type of behavior may even be described by some as blasphemous, sinful, or haram.

If this issue wasn't so prevalent, it wouldn't be such a fundamental curse to every other healthy parental effort we will be discussing throughout this book. If you skip this one and continue neglecting the need to rise to the occasion of Sound Parenting, everything else in this book will be far less effective. Next time your kid calls you "bruh," make sure to gently correct them, and you will slowly begin to reclaim both your authority and their respect.

The Origins of Sound Parenting

Our parenting journey began earlier than expected. Our son Kingston was born when I was 22 years old, just a week shy of our one-year wedding anniversary. As of this writing, Kingston is 16 and my daughter Saxyn is 14, both objectively amazing humans. I am extremely proud of both of them. If you have met them, you already agree, and in fact, meeting them might be the reason you are reading this book. I consider them the "proof-of-work" which led to compiling our strategies into these pages.

As a Bitcoiner, the descriptor of "sound money" has always resonated with me. I appreciate how the word doesn't work too hard to exaggerate or over promise on Bitcoin's prospects. Sound Parenting is similar in that there are no guarantees: proof-of-work is required and low-time preference is essential. This book is for all parents, but I hope readers within the emergent Bitcoin community, recently exploding with new births, will appreciate the subtle nods to Bitcoin throughout these pages. More importantly, I hope all readers will find value in the practical insights for how we've incorporated the basic principles of sound money into our methodology of Sound Parenting with our own kids.

Danielle and I are not extraordinary parents by any stretch. We've made plenty of mistakes and we'll continue to fall short from time to time. We will lose our temper, say something stupid, and even will apologize to our kids—like we have many times before. **We are imperfect humans raising imperfect humans with the active goal of seeing our kids become better versions of ourselves.** The goal of Sound Parenting isn't merely to have your kids "follow in your footsteps"—it is the aspiration to raise humans who exceed your own accomplishments and maturity. We want to see our children grow into high-character adults who can reduce the number of mistakes they make in this lifetime *despite* the shortcomings of their parents.

Danielle and I have been blessed to be on the same page with every one of these Sound Parenting tactics I'm sharing throughout this book. I imagine if one of us weren't aligned, they would be far less effective as we'd be in a constant power struggle to assert our respective will for what we thought was best. I recognize that not everyone reading this is parenting their children alongside a spouse who shares their vision (or even alongside a spouse at all). I acknowledge that I have no idea what that's like, and can only imagine the added stress, difficulty, and uncertainty this creates. I hope to offer something of value in these pages despite the unique challenges you are facing. It's only in hindsight that I can truly appreciate my wife, as well as the value of having two parents who sacrificed so much to ensure that my sisters and I had every opportunity to realize our dreams. Much of what I've learned is owed to the genuine love, care, and affection they consistently expressed to us. Regardless of the context you find yourself in as a parent, you're sure to make an impact if you are guided by those values.

Go, Set, Ready: How to Use This Book

While it can be challenging to form new habits, there are a few baby steps I want to suggest as you dive into this book. The first is to reorient your posture toward a bias for action by adopting a "Go, Set, Ready" mindset. Take immediate action with the parenting keys that resonate with you the most. Then, refine and iterate as you go until you begin to master new habits in your parenting that prove to be effective. If you overthink the suggestions or try to have it "all figured out" before you feel ready to act, chances are you will remain stuck. There is nothing more debilitating than waiting until you're ready before taking the next step you already know you must take.

The next piece of advice is even more essential: WRITE IT DOWN. Take notes. Create checklists. Develop your own ideas as inspiration strikes and build on the experiences I'm sharing throughout these pages by writing down your own actionable insights. As the saying goes, "if you fail to plan, you plan to fail." This is 100% accurate and parenting is no exception. You will not accidentally fall into solid parenting habits without committing to creating and implementing a written plan. I've included some suggested action steps at the end of each section which are meant to get the juices flowing on how to make practical use of the advice in this book. But if you merely read these suggestions and fly through this book without a written plan of action, you can expect very few of these insights to stick for any meaningful length of time. Write down as much as you can, review what you wrote, and commit to taking action while the information is fresh.

Personally, I write everything down somewhat obsessively. I have a physical day planner which serves as my system of record, to-do list, habit tracker, note taker, and historical log. I've done this for many years to the point where I can now search my own archives if I'm trying to recall where I was, what I was doing, and sometimes even what state of mind I might have been in during a noteworthy time of my life. You don't need to be this intense, but this critical suggestion relies on you demonstrating some "proof-of-work."

The following pages contain a collection of hard-fought lessons we've accumulated on this incredible journey of shepherding our children as they navigate the everyday struggles, triumphs, and questions of life. I hope this book is a helpful guide that offers easy-to-implement lessons, talking points, and best practices that we know have worked for us over the years. This book is for any parent or aspiring parent. I believe it can be beneficial to those with babies on the way all the way up to those with children entering the teenage years. I won't pretend to know much beyond that timeframe, so if your kids are already well past puberty, God bless you and best of luck. Perhaps there will be an empty nesters sequel, but for now we'll stay in our lane and stick to what we know.

Last thing: I'm primarily writing this book and will be the default voice throughout, but along the way I'm inviting Danielle, Kingston, and Saxyn to make contributions, edits, and offer feedback. So on behalf of Team Mekhail, we hope you find value in these 21 Keys to Sound Parenting and trust they will serve you and your family as they have served us.

—G.

SECTION 1
You've Got Kids!

In this section we confront the sobering reality of becoming, coping with, and celebrating parenthood. It starts with the simple acknowledgment that everything in your world is now different. There was life before kids, and now there is life after kids. By simply embracing this fact, you can begin to fully step into the responsibility of being a real-life parent of little humans. This will require an examination of how life's distractions frequently get in the way of being fully present with our children and how often we forget to slow down and simply enjoy the gift of parenthood.

In the first three chapters we'll explore the initial keys to Sound Parenting, which begin to lay the foundation for one of our primary goals—the intentional character development of our children. As we unpack the importance of Showing Up and Practicing Self-Awareness, you'll notice a decent portion of the advice is focused on the posture, attitude, and habits that you, the parent, carry into your daily interactions with your children. As Michael Jackson famously sang, "I'm starting with the man in the mirror / I'm asking him to change his ways." Who knew this would turn out to be sage parenting advice? At the end of the day, if we hope to find success in our parenting, we must first look inward and examine our own behaviors. I invite you to pay special attention to the dynamic between advice that is applicable to parents and the tools which are meant to be more prescriptive in day-to-day parenting. In many cases, both feed each other, reinforcing their core messages.

Throughout this section we'll also begin unpacking some useful mantras—not just the meaning behind them but the impact we've seen by utilizing them consistently in the Mekhail household. Prepare for some introspection, acronyms, and simple reminders as we explore the most basic yet always sobering realization for every parent: You've Got Kids!

CHAPTER 1
PARENTAL PRESENCE IS A PRESENT

C ongratulations! You've Got Kids. Whether they were planned or arrived in a more surprising fashion, they are all yours. You are responsible for raising the next generation. This responsibility must be fully appreciated in measurable ways, multiple times a day. One of the greatest gifts you can offer your children is your presence. Not just your physical presence—I'm talking about bringing your whole entire being into every interaction. These moments are precious, and you only get one shot to be the mother or father of your three-year-old. Once they turn four, you never get that previous phase back. Not only that, but they will never get your presence back for each stage of life they progress through.

We live in a fast-paced world full of a million distractions. Life is hard, and most people have a difficult enough time taking care of themselves and tending to their own priorities. Throw a whole additional human being into the mix—or multiple—and now all the sudden life feels like pure chaos most of the time. Welcome to parenting! All the weight of the simple day-to-day distractions and duties of adulting can make it easy to mail it in when it comes to being fully present with your children. It's much easier to let YouTube raise your kids than it is to actively engage with them. It can be tempting to scroll Instagram or check your email while your kid is telling you a story and chalk it up to multitasking. However, this habit of split focus is in fact an abdication of duty. By regularly deprioritizing your child, you are not-so-subtly communicating their level of importance relative to whatever else it is that has you captivated. There are limited exceptions to this basic rule of thumb. While there are of course real emergencies and urgent matters that need to be attended to before you can offer your full presence, be cautious of over-using this excuse. For the most part, the responsibility of parenting must naturally supersede just about everything else.

The biggest challenge of parenting is that there is no off switch. From the first fateful cry to whatever stage you currently find yourself in, being a parent is quite literally non-stop. Rather than resist this reality, I encourage you to embrace it wholeheartedly. Being fully engaged means tuning out the world and listening to what your child is saying. Focus on connecting, rather than controlling. It means asking relevant questions and thoughtful follow-up questions. It also means developing the skill of picking up on subtle signals that invite you into even deeper and more meaningful connections. I know this won't sound revolutionary, but actually *talking* to your kids has become somewhat of a lost art. Many parents have relegated themselves to becoming glorified babysitters, simply caring for the basic human needs of their offspring while neglecting to actually *be* with their kids in a meaningful way. This is tragic. If you do not seek out real conversation and if you are not genuinely interested, you will not automatically fall into the habit of bringing your full self when engaging with your children. This simple requirement of Sound Parenting emphasizes the importance of the golden rule: treating your children the way you would want to be treated when you are sharing a story, seeking attention, or asking someone a question.

The Present Moment

I have this obsession with the present moment. Often during dinner, the question of "What was your favorite part of the day?" comes up. My response to this question without fail has been, "My favorite part of the day is right now because it's happening in the present moment." I realize this is a bit cheesy, but this small tactic has become an incredibly powerful teaching opportunity because it emphasizes the value of right *now*. Even as you read these words, I believe there is enormous power in becoming aware that you are here, in the present moment, intentionally seeking answers to parenting. It can be a holy moment if you allow it to be. Try this: take a deep breath and appreciate the magnitude of simply being alive. Wow! Isn't it crazy that breathing is free? I mean, at least for now the government hasn't found a way to tax air, so enjoy it. This practice of returning to the present moment has become invaluable for me personally and has significantly impacted my approach to parenting. Dwelling on the past is typically unhelpful and worrying about the future often creates anxiety. It is only in the here and now that we are alive.

Reflecting on the magnitude of life as it takes place in the present moment can significantly shape how you interact with your children. It helps you slow down and pay attention to every detail of their development. You start noticing small mannerisms, habits, and personalities unfolding right before your eyes. This is your parental payday. Becoming more patient and focused on your duty to teach them everything you know and guide them through the ups and downs of daily life starts to come more naturally. You start prioritizing the importance of making memories and ensuring they are set up to succeed in every aspect you are able to provide. As basic as it sounds, this truly is a bit of a secret weapon, but it's not easy. It may even require a complete reorientation of your outlook and perhaps a bit of spiritual contemplation. I challenge you to give it a shot and see how things begin to change and how life becomes a bit sweeter as you slow down and take in the present moment. Honestly, if you get nothing else out of this book, I hope this paragraph offers a gentle nudge in a direction that I believe will bear much fruit. Be here now—for yourself and your children.

YOUR KIDS ARE NOT A BURDEN

I get a little triggered when I hear parents habitually complaining about their kids. This practice might be the only thing worse than trying to be best friends with your kids. Please, I beg of you, stop doing this altogether. Regardless of how difficult your children might be, their existence is not a burden. Even if they are unplanned, they are not an inconvenience.

Every child is a miracle because life itself is miraculous. When parents continually complain about their kids or about having kids, all sorts of red flags fly for me. Not only is it an obvious sign of immaturity, it can also become an incredibly powerful self-fulfilling prophecy. Similar to the dynamics of self-talk (which we'll discuss later), if we adopt phrases like, "Harold is such a difficult little hellion," we are putting that out into the universe in ways we often underestimate. Not only have we vocalized it, we've also likely internalized it as a true statement. We are now orienting our approach to little Harold through this particular lens, and what's worse is we're sowing questionable seeds in the minds of others within earshot about Harold's character—not to mention underestimating the amount of time Harold himself has overheard your said complaints.

I am not suggesting denying reality or giving Harold excuses for unsavory behavior. I imagine there are elements of truth behind the complaint. However, the first thing to recognize is that the apple doesn't fall far from the tree. More than likely, the hellion within you is creating a hellion in your offspring. The second thing to recognize is that no child is perfect and whatever frustration you are dealing with in your life as a parent is family business. I get it; there are times you want to vent after a long, challenging day of struggling with your child. But the habit of airing out your parental complaints is a close cousin of gossip, with the primary victim being your child.

To take this a step further, it is simply not enough to avoid complaining about your kid. They are not background characters in your story that must be tolerated because you're responsible for ensuring they stay alive. We must replace these mindsets with their positive counterparts, which means finding ways to celebrate your kids. Every improvement or display of a desired character trait is cause for celebration. I'm talking about celebrating actual progress, not manufactured wins. The point isn't to award trophies for losses or try to make kids feel good for the sake of protecting their self-confidence. But when you do experience moments of true progress, it's important to take the time to intentionally acknowledge those parental victories. This form of "gossip" is encouraged and can be a helpful tactic to replace a posture of habitual complaining. Don't just tolerate—celebrate.

It's instructive to recognize that periodic faults or mistakes, which are often the subject of parental gossip, do not equate to poor character. There are times when external reasons create attitude, tantrums, laziness, lack of follow-through, etc. Are they overstimulated? Did they have a bad day? Sometimes harboring something inside eats away at them to where all you see (and in turn communicate) is the negative outcome of some deeper dynamic that is playing out. When we habitually complain about our kids, it's easy to omit the underlying context. What's worse is failing to understand the underlying context. By slowing down and intentionally being present, we can more easily uncover what's going on beneath the surface. This in turn will lead to a reduced amount of complaining and create more opportunities to celebrate.

An Attitude of Gratitude

One last point of emphasis on parental presence is the importance of gratitude. This again stems from slowing down and living life in the present moment, but it is an additional step that can be easily overlooked, especially if you are experiencing hardships and struggles. Even if life is great now and seemingly smooth sailing, one thing is certain: you will at some point face trials and difficulties. I find it best to prepare for those when things are going well so that you are adequately equipped when conditions change for the worse. Adopting a posture of gratitude for the small things is a contagious habit. If you are simply grateful for another day of being alive, you will notice people around you begin to reflect that gratitude back to you in their own demeanor. At the end of the day, life is an inexplicable miracle. The mystery of what it all means—what we are doing here and where we are going can—be anxiety-inducing at times. **I believe gratitude is the natural antidote for existential dread**. No one likes a constant doomer. No one likes a whiner (I dedicate an entire chapter to this later). When a person is full of genuine hope and thankfulness, people tend to gravitate toward their energy and it becomes infectious. I'm not talking about "fake it 'til you make it" Pollyanna optimism. I'm talking about simple, authentic, resilience rooted in gratitude and an abundance mentality.

Anthony Pompliano, better known as "Pomp" is a well-known media personality and financial guru who starts every day with a simple tweet: Good morning. Today is going to be a great day. Let's get after it relentlessly.

I always smile when I see this tweet in my feed. It's a simple set of words, sent daily with an extremely valuable underlying message. It contains a positive outlook, reminder to focus, encouragement to work hard, and is delivered consistently for maximum effect. It's the type of attitude I want to surround myself with and the kind of energy I want to infuse into my children. There is plenty of negativity out there, so if that seeps into the home too frequently, then kids have nowhere to turn to for a more hopeful, inspiring message. Life becomes daunting and struggles seem insurmountable without a consistent flicker of light at the end of the tunnel.

At the end of the day, all of these recommendations are about character development. Your thoughts become your actions, which become your habits, culminating in becoming your character. With every passing moment you are either inching closer to actualizing the person you want to be or you are drifting toward falling short of your God-given potential. The same is true of how you guide your children. The choice is yours, but it really does start with you.

CHAPTER 2
SHOWING UP

At the Mekhail Family homeschool, my wife does basically everything. Recently, however, I've started teaching a weekly class covering a variety of life-skill topics, including Managing Disagreements, Bitcoin (obviously), and Scarcity versus Abundance. But the most popular teaching I have shared is Showing Up! My thesis is simple: how you show up significantly shapes your character.

Every day in every moment and with every decision, whether consciously or subconsciously, you are becoming someone. The question is whether or not you like the person you are becoming. The level of intentionality that is required to truly shape one's character cannot be overstated. It requires having clear goals and aspirations. It also requires focus, commitment, and self-control. When I talk about Showing Up, I'm referring to the literal act of being a human being in the world, especially when you are in the presence of other people. Sure, it is also good practice to show up when you're by yourself, especially when we're talking about actively working toward a goal, but the reality is you can't always be *on*—there is a need to simply rest. Do not fear: I have a wonderful acronym to unpack what this key means and how to practically apply it to your daily life and in turn, how to instruct your children to follow suit. I refer to this delicious acronym as APPIE:

Awareness

Presence

Preparation

Intentionality

Energy

AWARENESS

There are two primary types of awareness: self-awareness (which we'll cover next chapter) and situational awareness. Both are relevant to the practice of Showing Up, but the latter is perhaps more critical, especially in social situations. You want your kids to value the importance of scanning their environment and being aware of their surroundings. This is not only helpful for safety but also instructive in terms of how you move about in any given setting. Awareness informs the behavior, language, or even dress code which is most appropriate for the environment. By acknowledging these distinctions exist, there is a bit of freedom that is granted in teaching kids how to show up depending on the context.

This isn't about being fake from setting to setting, but it is a simple recognition of the fact that different environments have different rules, if you will. Some people might refer to this as "code switching." Whatever you want to call it, I believe it is an incredibly helpful skill to learn from an early age, which serves you well into adulthood. Some conversations which are appropriate at home may not be appropriate at school. You wear a swimsuit to a pool party, but probably not to a Christmas party. You get the picture. Being aware of your environment takes practice, but once taught, it can serve as the ultimate confidence boost by enabling you to be firmly grounded wherever you find yourself.

PRESENCE

We unpacked the importance of parental presence in depth in the previous chapter, so I won't belabor the point here. However, in the context of Showing Up, it is a helpful reminder to bring your whole self to the particular environment you are entering. This is as simple as not being on your phone when you are hanging out IRL with other people (a topic that probably deserves an entire book unto itself). Put your phone down, turn your notifications off, and show up. This also extends to being mentally present and attempting to leave other concerns behind in order to be able to fully engage with whatever it is you are about to do. Presence shapes character because it impacts your relationships with other people. It is obvious to others when you are "somewhere else" mentally or emotionally, even when you are standing right in front of them physically. The truth is, if you can't or don't want to be fully present in a given environment, there is a deeper question lurking about what you are even doing there to begin with. This is a valid question. It's healthy to reflect on the reason for being absent-minded and teach your kids that in many cases, maybe it's worth reconsidering whether or not they want to put themselves in that situation in the future. Either way, just as your presence as a parent is a gift, your simple presence as a human is also a gift to those around you, and remaining present is a key aspect of Showing Up.

Preparation

Almost everything on your calendar can benefit from some proactive preparation prior to proceeding. Listen, I know you came for the acronyms, but I'm glad you also stayed for the alliteration. To quote NFL quarterback Russell Wilson, "The separation is in the preparation." These are the facts. To properly show up, you must prepare. This might mean studying, doing research, or even meditating. Depending on what you're about to get yourself into, you can exponentially increase your impact with even a little effort ahead of time. The more time and energy you are able to invest into preparing, the more you can properly enter into a new environment with focus and poise. Getting in the habit of helping your kids prepare is an incredibly effective practice of Sound Parenting. They need time to get into the correct mental state, wrap up loose ends, and adjust their attitude according to the nature of the impending transition. A practical approach to helping your kids prepare is to plant seeds early and often about what they can expect on a given day. Saying, "Harold, don't forget we are going to Aunt Ruth's house after soccer practice, so it's going to be a busy day!" goes a long way in allowing young Harold to adjust his expectations and mentally prepare for a disruption to his typical routine. Abrupt context switching can be even more taxing on children than on adults, so be mindful and anticipate their need to prepare, especially on days packed full of activities and transitions.

INTENTIONALITY

I love this word. I'm curious to see how many times I end up using it throughout this book. Believe it or not, I'm using this word a lot on purpose (see what I did there?). Being intentional means thinking through your purpose, what you want, and what you can bring to any given situation. It is the opposite of winging it. Similar in some ways to preparation, but distinct in that it is the outworking or the implementation of the preparation. People who have commendable character are consistently intentional with the way they spend their time and the way they go about their business. They move around their environments with a noticeable sense of purpose and confidence. They know who they are and where they are going. It is a key attribute to teach your children, and it pays dividends to prioritize modeling and teaching this skill yourself. One aspect of cultivating intentionality starts with curiosity and self-reflection. You must first know what you want in order to set out to intentionally achieve it. It's amazing how often we coast through life, going through the motions and allowing routines and habits to chart our path. In order to break out of these common patterns, we have to choose to be people of clear intent and teach our children to do likewise. Don't overthink it. It can really be as simple as setting attainable goals, creating realistic to-do lists of desired milestones or tasks, and regularly reflecting on your progress. By increasing intentionality, you may even notice your calendar begin to free up as you eliminate commitments that do not serve your goals. Stop doing things just to do them, and stop signing your kids up for things to "keep them busy" or "because we've always done it" or some other random, thoughtless reason. It's almost impossible to show up effectively if the activity, event, or environment isn't entered into with purpose.

ENERGY

By now you might have noticed how each of these APPIEs build on each other and are somewhat interdependent. Perhaps the most important aspect of Showing Up is doing so with energy. You know who the least interesting person is in any social situation? The person who responds to, "How you doin?" with, "I'm tired." Boring! Expel this phrase from your vocabulary and teach your kids to do likewise. This useless phrase is a close cousin of "I'm bored" and "I don't know." We will dive deeper into words in the next section, but the point here is that high energy is closely related to high character. It's tough to be energetic and enthusiastic about life if you have very little to be excited about. I'm raising kids who are dynamic and draw people to themselves anytime they are in a room. This starts with the simple habit of smiling, looking people in the eyes, shaking hands, and kissing babies. It may be that charisma is genetic—I'm not sure. I can only assume that it's at least partially taught and with enough effort and genuine excitement about life, anyone can develop a level of magnetism that is simply helpful in just about any situation. Next time someone asks how you're doing, take a few beats and consider the question. Give an interesting answer that they are not expecting. Deliver it with confidence and swagger. Don't let life happen to you—go out there and take life by the horns. Carpe diem! Add up these habits of Showing Up and you will be unstoppable in life, full of confidence, and ready to take on whatever challenges await—with your children looking to you as an example to emulate.

Do As I Do

The skill of Showing Up, like most other keys we're exploring, starts with you, the parent. You are a mirror and your kids are watching your every move. As you show up, they will show up. One of the worst phrases a parent can utter is, "Do as I say, not as I do." If anything, the opposite advice contains more wisdom. With every move you make, you are modeling for your children what is appropriate and desirable behavior. If you're always complaining about how tired you are, guess what? Little Alfred is suddenly going to be tired a lot more. Teach your kids to show up, but also pay attention to how you're Showing Up. If you're at a social gathering and you notice your child is disengaged, the temptation is to go ask them what's wrong and try to coax them into participating in whatever is taking place. Sound Parenting proposes a different approach. You take the lead in how you're Showing Up and go out of your way to demonstrate what they are missing out on, which is of course the present moment. This may or may not work at this hypothetical pity party, but either way it provides you with a powerful talking point on the drive home. It's okay to let them sulk for a single event if you capitalize on the learning opportunity after the fact. Don't let it go to waste. Talk to them about Showing Up, but make sure you do so without being hypocritical and while being able to point to the way you are Showing Up. "Do as I do" becomes the more instructive and helpful mantra.

The essential habit of Showing Up is once again rooted in situational awareness. Helping your children practice all the APPIE skills will go a long way in accelerating their maturity and confidence. We now turn to the closely related topic, which is less about the environments we walk into and more about being in tune with who we are and what's going on inside of us as we navigate this crazy apocalyptic world.

CHAPTER 3
PRACTICE SELF-AWARENESS

It's time to get a little meta.

Who are you? Where did you come from? What are you doing here? What do you want? Where are you going? All of these questions require deep reflection and consideration, and they begin nagging every human being from a very early age. Best believe your kids are already asking themselves these questions—maybe not verbally, but for sure within the quiet of their own soul. One of your most critical tasks is not only helping them discover the answers to these questions but also encouraging them to embrace part of the mystery that the questions themselves contain. The truth is some (if not all) of these thought-provoking questions are impossible to answer in a way that is conclusive and satisfying. The human experience is about the journey, not necessarily about the destination. So while you may be able to partially answer some of these questions for a season of life, chances are you will reach a point where the question you once considered settled will begin to emerge all over again. How exhausting! A helpful way to effectively navigate these universally confounding questions is the practice of self-awareness.

For as long as I can remember, we've instilled the persistent encouragement of practicing self-awareness with our kids and it continues to serve as a cornerstone of our parenting to this day. Being self-aware is another attribute of high-character individuals. To illustrate what self-awareness looks like, it might be helpful to consider the opposite quality of being aloof. People who lack self-awareness are easy to spot. They are usually disruptive, annoying, or socially awkward. They might lack self-confidence, say or do inappropriate things, or be inconsiderate to those around them. These are not desirable qualities, and when compounded can result in overall poor character, which can be difficult to reverse. The goal of teaching self-awareness is to help kids hold up a mirror and allow them to see on their own what they had previously failed to see.

YOU PROBABLY THINK THIS CHAPTER'S ABOUT YOU

There's a slippery slope here that I want to address, which is becoming self-indulgent or vain. As with most of the keys of Sound Parenting we're exploring, there is a delicate balance between a desired outcome and an over-emphasis or obsession with it (which ultimately distracts from the actual goal). This is a critical distinction and a common trap parents fall into when instructing their children. In the case of self-awareness, **I make a clear distinction between *caring* about what people think versus *worrying* about what people think.** It's a subtle but critical difference. Hot take: it's okay to care about what people think. You live in a world with other humans, and it's selfish and foolish to maintain an attitude of, "Oh, I don't care what people think of me." I also find that when people say this, they rarely mean it. Of course you care. You care what the hiring manager thinks at your interview. You care what the teacher thinks before a parent-teacher conference. You care what the girl you have a crush on thinks of you. I hate to break it to you, but you care what people think, whether you want to admit it or not.

Often what I believe people are intending to communicate is a much healthier version of the same phrase, which is, "I'm not *worried* about what people think." Now we're talking. The reality is you cannot control what people think of you. You can only hope to influence their impression of you, which may or may not be accurate, and it may or may not matter. When you *worry* about what people think, that's when you risk beginning to conform to other people's expectations, capitulating to peer pressure, or sacrificing your integrity and self-respect in order to please others. This is the opposite of living into the essence of who you were created to be and it is a fast pass to falling short of your potential. Worrying about what people think is unhealthy and leads to self-destructive behavior. Care, but don't worry. The former is self-awareness, the latter is self-consciousness.

By now you may be asking yourself what the value is of even *caring* what people think. Valid question. In many ways, this goes back to the golden rule: if everyone acted purely out of their own self-interest all of the time without considering how their behavior affects others around them, society would suffer. One could argue that is exactly what is taking place in our modern world. Basic human decency calls for a level of consideration and cooperation with our fellow man. The Bible refers to this as loving your neighbor as yourself. Once again, taking this logic to its extreme is not the goal. We're not looking for complete self-immolation or disregard for one's aspirations, dreams, and pursuits in favor of making others happy. Believe it or not, it is possible to maintain a healthy balance of being considerate while not neglecting your own needs, desires, and passions. Practicing self-awareness effectively can create a virtuous flywheel in our world, especially if parents model this and pass the wisdom down to their children.

What's in Your Hand?

The lead-up to the Biblical Exodus is intense. I mean, let's be honest—the whole Bible is intense. But a passage I continually return to is Exodus 4:2, which says:

> Then the Lord said to Moses, "What is that in your hand?"

> "A staff," he replied.

You remember what happens next: God tells him to throw it on the ground, it turns into a snake, Moses freaks out, God tells him to pick it up, so he does, and it turns back into a staff. This staff is then used multiple times throughout the Exodus saga and is eventually the very same tool that Moses uses to part the Red Sea. Now, I realize that depending on your view of the Bible, you may consider this story to be a historical account, an allegory, or even a fabrication. Hit pause on those opinions for now because the story can be instructive regardless of your biblical cosmology. The reason I like to recall the question "What's in your hand?" is because it provides an excellent self-reflection prompt and can help lead to greater self-awareness. Another way you see it asked is, "What skills, talents, gifts, resources, connections, visions, or traits do you possess?" What can you do with them with even just a little faith? It's helpful to revisit these questions from time to time, especially in moments where you or your children are feeling down or lacking confidence. Consider where Moses' headspace was right before God asked him this question:

Moses answered, "What if they do not believe me or listen to me..." (Exodus 4:1).

In other words, he's feeling apprehensive and unsure of himself, unable to muster the energy to show up and be a leader. The antidote here is God's simple inquiry: "What's that you got in your hot little hand Moses?" I'm going to go out on a limb here and suggest that we all have more than we realize and possess several quality traits we often neglect to give ourselves proper credit for. This condition is even more pronounced in young children who often feel inadequate when they measure themselves against their siblings, their peers, or their favorite YouTuber. It can be helpful to use prompts or questions like this to allow your children to arrive at their own conclusions, rather than simply telling them or reminding them of how great they are or all the things they have to be thankful for when they are feeling down. Your role is to nudge them to use their own brain and hone these skills to invest in their own self-development. Ask your offspring, "What's in your hand?" explain what you mean, and watch the wheels start turning (this method is also one of the best ways to generate curiosity about biblical stories if that is of interest to you). Sometimes just reading the story and letting it speak for itself unlocks incredible value that can stick with you in unique ways.

Sorry, Heather

When Saxyn was about 10 years old, she asked if she could get a TikTok account. As you can probably imagine, upon first review it was a hard "no" from her mother and me. This was also back when every TikTok video was either a Charli D'Amelio dance video or some iteration of the "Martha dump truck in the flesh" meme. Over the course of the next several weeks, Saxyn took the approach of asking thoughtful questions and was on a tactical mission of getting Danielle and me on board with her request. She was extremely patient and respectful, but she was also very methodical in navigating our objections. I couldn't help but be impressed. The more we listened, the more her ask began to sound somewhat reasonable. It turned out she simply wanted to upload screen recordings of her gameplay of a popular Roblox game called *Adopt Me*. She wasn't asking to show her face, reveal her voice, or anything that would personally identify who she was or her age. The combination of these factors, her level of maturity, and with the acceptance of a few other conditions (such as keeping us informed and providing us full access to the account) led to us eventually conceding, and a new Roblox fan page was born. Spoiler Alert: her account ended up exploding. She quickly gained about 25,000 followers and often found herself managing hundreds of comments on her posts—unexpected outcomes that no one (not even Saxyn) really anticipated.

A few months float by before things started spiraling out of control. Her TikTok fame increasingly began to require more of her time, energy, and creativity to keep up with the feverish fan base she now commanded. What started as an innocent desire to share some fun videos was suddenly a burden and a bit of a responsibility that Saxyn didn't exactly sign up for. One day she came downstairs and announced, "I deleted my TikTok account." We were all stunned. Speechless. I do not know many people who can grow a social account to that many followers, that quickly, let alone possess the conviction and self-awareness to delete it when it ceases to give them joy. I still think about the level of maturity it took to decide to delete that account, forgo the attention and dopamine hits it was providing, and move on to the next thing with relative ease. But at the end of the day, Saxyn understood the tradeoffs with a level of self-awareness that still amazes me and makes me proud. She also understood that the very skills, talent, and creativity she possessed, which generated that level of success with a silly TikTok Roblox fan account, were squarely located in her hand. This is the power of acutely tuned self-awareness.

CHAPTER 4
Make Good Choices, Be Good Leaders

⊶

I started using this phrase as my final words to the kids when dropping them off at elementary school and I continue to use it to this day as they are getting ready to go hang out with friends or leave the house. Danielle and I frequently talk about one of our primary intentions with parenting is raising kids who are becoming leaders. The concept of leadership in our world has become somewhat elusive if not straight up confusing. Leadership is not the same as authority and it's not the same as popularity. Just because you are President of the United States, it doesn't make you a leader, or at the very least, it doesn't automatically make you an imitable leader. Being a celebrity also doesn't equate to being a leader worthy of following, even though many celebrities boast countless "fans" following them on social media, watching their every move in the tabloids, or even admiring them as role models. Effective leadership has become the only thing in this world scarcer than Bitcoin.

The unfortunate state of affairs in our modern era can be directly linked to a lack of effective leadership. The people in power are largely consumed by greed, control, and corruption. This is partly due to a woefully misaligned incentive structure exacerbated by a broken monetary system, which allows the rich to easily become richer and the corrupt to accelerate unchecked in their corruption. We'll explore this topic in more depth later, but it's almost as if things have gotten so bad that those who occupy positions of power are no longer even concerned about optics. They are flaunting and taunting their oppression as if to say, "What are you going to do about it?"

I believe part of the answer to that question requires playing the long game through Sound Parenting. If the next generation of parents commits to a vision of raising up the next generation of strong leaders, we will begin to make meaningful progress in humanity's shared struggle for the ideals of freedom, peace, and prosperity. If you consider every historic breakthrough during periods where humans have fought back and emerged victorious when faced with tyranny, you will find examples of strong leadership. At the end of the day, someone's gotta raise the next George Washington, and there's no reason that can't be me or you.

Take Yourself Seriously

I find it funny when people say, "Don't take yourself so seriously." It's like, how am I supposed to take myself then? I'm a fairly lighthearted individual; I like to make people laugh: I can also be over the top with my positive attitude. Life's too short, begging to be taken by the horns and shaped into my every hope and dream. In that sense, I would say I do take myself seriously. If you don't take yourself seriously, you certainly shouldn't expect anyone else to take you seriously. And what a bummer way to live this one precious life. I say: take yourself seriously. Have lofty goals. Dream big. Fail often. Show up. Keep moving forward. Laugh loudly. Take risks. Be extra. Don't hedge. And most importantly: teach your children to do likewise. Don't listen to the insecurities of others who need you to shrink down so they can feel better about themselves. Don't stifle dreams before they even have a chance to see the light of day. The world needs more boldness, more fearlessness, and more outliers who are not afraid to stand up to bullshit. I guarantee you that every legendary historical figure took themselves seriously, took their dreams seriously, and went about their business very seriously. Make no mistake, this is an active, ongoing, continual decision that requires constant self-reflection and self-awareness. It requires not *worrying* about what people think of you. Every time you decide to take yourself seriously, you are taking steps to not only achieving your goals, but also fulfilling your God-given potential.

TAKE RESPONSE + ABILITY

Each of our lives can be boiled down to a series of decisions. Every day we are becoming someone, and the person we are becoming is made up of the choices we make. With every circumstance we face, we can decide: how will I navigate this? It is our response to every question that emerges, whether it's expected, fair, or difficult. The truth is we are each equipped with the ability to evaluate these situations and decide the best course of action. The combination of utilizing our abilities to respond appropriately demonstrates one of the most beautiful words in the English language: responsibility. Seriously, can we just take a moment to appreciate how rich this word is and how consequential it is in this game of life?

Making good choices and being good leaders requires taking responsibility. Teaching our children how to take responsibility for their life is a foundational goal of quality parenting. The baby steps to achieving this outcome start with helping them recognize the real-world impact of every decision. To zoom out even further, it's helping them see how much of their present situation boils down to the numerous decisions they've already made. Yes, everyone has different abilities. Yes, everyone has different response tools at their disposal. But by the same token, everyone has the opportunity to embrace their own set of responsibilities based on their given circumstances. The mark of effective leadership is found in one's willingness to carry greater responsibility than what would otherwise be reasonably expected of them. Strong leaders crave responsibility and tend to seek it out proactively. In turn, they also have a propensity to make wise, thoughtful, and intentional decisions in every situation they face.

On the flip side, poor decision-making can be described as an inability to effectively respond to a given situation. Let's call it response-inability for fun. This is often a hallmark of not only poor leaders but also those who we might describe as sheeple, NPCs, or blind followers. Consider how many poor decisions are made as a result of "peer pressure" or "following orders." These are not the type of kids we are trying to raise. We want lions, not sheep. The world is sadly inundated with uncritical thinkers who are raising uncritical thinking kids who lack the tools to embrace responsibility—and who would rather have someone else make decisions for them. Poor decisions tend to compound, sadly much faster than wise decisions. Once this momentum gets going, you have a recipe for outcomes like addiction, pain, and ultimately regret.

No Regrets When You're 80

As far as we know, we only live once. There will only ever be one George Samir Naguib Mekhail Saad Nasir Massoud. As much as it would be helpful to have, there is no undo button in life. You can't command Z your way through existence. "No regrets when you're 80" is more of a personal refrain I've adopted, but I've used it with my kids to help illustrate the implications and importance of mindful decision-making and numbering your days. We all have regrets; things we wish we would have done differently or things we wish we could change. I approach the idea of regret as strictly describing something that is literally unchangeable. Oftentimes we ascribe the word regret to situations that can actually be changed but would be very difficult or require a lot of discomfort to actualize said change. Some people will say, "I regret the way things went with Justine," when in reality, they can pick up the phone and give ol' Justine a call to mend a relationship. You might not need to give her a call today, but perhaps sometime before you're 80 you can eliminate at least one regret from your list. I call this mantra to mind when I'm faced with a particularly large decision in order to help me put the options into perspective. The question behind the phrase is: if I decide to do X, what is the likelihood that I will regret this decision when I'm near the end of my life?

It's helpful to note that the idea of avoiding regret can devolve into an unhealthy obsession, which may cause one to limit risk-taking and expressing creativity. This is not what I'm proposing. Rather, we must find a healthy balance when it comes to limiting situations where irreversible regret is created. Most critically, we must coach our children on the importance of their decision-making early in life and help them understand how these decisions will compound, like interest, over time. The sooner our kids learn to take responsibility for every action in life, the more mature, wise, and self-reliant they will become. Good decisions lead to outstanding character. Outstanding character produces excellent leaders. Excellent leaders, raise children who exceed them in every category because that was the goal all along.

CHAPTER 5
WATCH YOUR SELF-TALK

Self-talk is the verbal manifestation of our inner dialogue, and it heavily influences our emotions, confidence, and ultimately our actions. Whether in the positive sense, as in "I am amazing," or in a negative sense, as in "I am stupid," self-talk is a potent weapon that can either do significant harm or assist in defeating mental enemies. For this reason, we developed the persistent mantra, "Watch your self-talk," in the Mekhail home, and we utilize it quite frequently for both accountability and encouragement.

The entire notion of self-talk is common sense, but because habitual self-talk seems to be prevalent, it is worth spending some time unpacking why it's important. You know how when you get a new car, you suddenly start noticing the same car on the road more frequently? Or when you learn a new word, it seems to start popping up everywhere in conversation? The one-two punch of Practicing Self-Awareness and

Watching Your Self-Talk might have a similar effect. My goal in this chapter is to first highlight how frequently negative self-talk persists, and then encourage swift correction when it appears.

The power of self-talk lies in its ability to influence our self-perception and consequently our behavior. Any verbal expression about ourselves, characterized by positivity, encouragement, and self-compassion, can serve as a powerful motivator and a source of resilience. On the other hand, negative self-talk can be a detrimental force, eroding self-esteem and leading to perennial self-doubt. It can create a self-fulfilling prophecy by reinforcing limiting beliefs and sabotaging our true potential.

The biggest problem with negative self-talk is it's often not even factually accurate. Not only are you verbalizing counterproductive descriptors of yourself but you are also telling yourself lies. Double whammy! When you say something like, "I am stupid," there is a good chance that's not the case. You're probably somewhat smart or maybe even highly intelligent. That said, I want to be clear that I'm not proposing you teach your children to gloss over undesirable behavior or pretend like everything is perfect. What I am proposing is another subtle adjustment to the language that is used to describe these moments. Consider the difference between the phrases, "I'm so stupid!" and "Man, that was a stupid thing I just did." Yes, you might have done something stupid or said something stupid, but that does not mean that you are stupid. The distinction here is what separates negative self-talk from a more accurate and helpful description of reality.

Not With That Attitude

I'm militant about the attitude my kids carry if I'm being completely honest. Hearing my children utter self-deprecating words is like nails on a chalkboard to me. They might as well be dropping F-bombs. Whoever said, "Sticks and stones may break my bones, but words can never hurt me," was flat-out wrong. Words possess incredible power to inflict significant harm not just to our emotions, but to our psyche. If you habitually repeat phrases like, "Ugh, I can't do this!" you are actively increasing your chances of failure. One of my go-to quips in response to these types of negative expressions of self-talk is "Not with that attitude!"

> "I'm never going to figure this out!"—not with that attitude.

> "This is too hard, I can't do it!"—not with that attitude.

> "Traffic is horrible, there's no way I'm going to be on time!"—not with that attitude.

Okay, so maybe only the first two are helpful, but that last one serves as a great dad joke template from time to time. I am admittedly quick to offer corrections and redirect the energy to a more helpful framing. To be sure, I understand that sometimes things *are* in fact too hard and sometimes you *may not* be able to do it. Nonetheless, by infusing confidence into difficult situations, we can begin to significantly impact our mindset, resolve, and determination. Perhaps we fail the first three times, but we effectively hype ourselves up enough to give it another go and provide ourselves the opportunity to taste sweet success on the fourth go around. "I got this!" is simply more helpful than "I'm too dumb to figure this out." **The lies we verbalize about ourselves can very quickly become true if we do not keep our self-talk in check.** Teaching children this habit at an early age equals maximizing the time they have to develop healthy self-perception.

Comparison Is the Thief of Joy

Oftentimes negative self-talk can stem from comparing ourselves to others. Mothers panic when their child fails to walk, talk, or read before another. Not only does this stir up negativity within the parent, but it also permeates into the soul of their own offspring. Young kids can easily perceive when a sibling or a peer is "ahead" of them in some way, shape, or form. They will also tend to give up more easily if they notice that someone their age (or—heaven forbid—younger than them) is able to succeed in a given area with more ease than them, while they struggle to make progress. This dynamic can create unique challenges for children who are "late-bloomers" and really take a toll on their motivation if they are unable to develop tools to avoid the comparison trap. On the other hand, for children who seem to possess unusual talent, charisma, or skills beyond their years, comparison can still function as the thief of their joy. I've seen this manifest in a variety of ways. Sometimes the highly-capable child observes that their gifts make others insecure, and so they dumb it down in a noble but self-defeating effort to not make others feel bad about themselves. Less commendable is the extremely talented kid who knows they're gifted and lords it over his inferior peers, alienating himself and going out of his way to make sure others know how much better he is than they are. Both are familiar and neither are healthy. **They say "pride cometh before the fall," but when you are trained to live in the present moment, you begin to recognize that actively living out of pride is the fall itself.**

In our modern world, scrolling Instagram for a few minutes and seeing how "happy" and "successful" everyone is can plant not-so-subtle seeds of self-doubt and insecurity, which later manifest into verbalized self-deprecation and can tragically result in destructive behavior or habits. Your young children may not be on Instagram yet, but you won't be able to shelter them from the evolution of these technologies as they continue to grow. I find a more productive approach is to prepare them for these inevitabilities by helping them focus on what they can control to improve their situation or overcome obstacles, rather than looking outward for sources of affirmation. Unhealthy comparison games can rob us of our joy and violate our inner peace more often than it motivates us toward self-improvement. Life isn't zero-sum. Other people can win at life at the same time you are winning at life. Instagram is not reality.

WORRY ABOUT YOURSELF

Do you remember the popular YouTube video from several years ago where the young girl is getting herself buckled into her car seat while her dad is asking how he can help? She is intent on completing the task alone, even while she seems to be struggling and continues to reject her father's offer to help with the repeated and now viral catchphrase, "Worry about yourself!" Instant classic, one of the best—I just watched it again, amazing still to this day. Believe it or not, there is a lot of wisdom packed into this phrase that is relevant for our discussion here, and it's another phrase we've adopted along the way, deploying it strategically throughout the course of parenting. It's a helpful reminder when you find yourself falling into comparison games or falling into patterns of judgment of others. It's even more great for the household that has sibling rivalries and one sibling is constantly getting into the business of the other. Worry about yourself.

While the video is hilarious, and you must appreciate the cute, spontaneous moments in their context, I want to be clear that as parents, we have the obligation to in fact worry about our kids. So this isn't exactly a two-way street or a hall pass to allow your young children to play an Uno reverse card on you and hit you with a "Worry about yourself" when you ask them to get ready for bed. It IS a helpful barometer for parents to self-gauge in certain situations where they are abusing their authority, being overly nosey, gossiping, and so on. It is much more effective when modeled with actions first, lest it devolve into another version of, "Do as I say, not as I do." By worrying about yourself, and teaching your children to worry about themselves, we can begin to foster environments of self-reliance while reducing fear of judgment or allowing the pace or success of others to dictate our mindset and motivation. The first step to properly worry about yourself is getting your self-talk in check. From there, we can begin to consider how our character more acutely shapes our interactions and relationships to other humans.

CHAPTER 6
WE DON'T NAME-CALL

G rowing up with "George" as my first name opened me up to a fair amount of teasing. Kids would sing, "George, George, George of the Jungle," or randomly yell, "Watch out for that tree!" I felt subconscious about being curious for fear of being called "Curious George," which was tough because I'm naturally a curious person. The most common was the song, "Georgie Porgie Pudding and Pie, kissed the girls and made them cry," to which I eventually developed the response "for more" anytime someone would come at me with this classic. I thought I was clever.

Looking back, I realize this was mostly silly banter, but it likely contributed to my posture toward name-calling in general. Of course name-calling is petty and immature. In my mind, it is an immediate sign of weakness. Taking it upon yourself to use a negative label to describe another human being is a sign of poor character quality. Children often participate in petty name-calling because they lack the skills, vocabulary, and wisdom to engage at a level of greater maturity. On the playground, it can also be a bit of a contagious phenomenon. Saying to someone, "You're an idiot," or "You're a meanie head," does not add value to any interaction and is often counterproductive. The advent of the internet, especially Facebook, has only increased the need for this reminder. I see grown adults frivolously name-call celebrities or politicians they dislike. Beware of even minor slights and even more cautious of combining name-calling with absolutes (which we will discuss later). Phrases like, "You're always so rude!" are a great way to accelerate an argument and cause lasting relational damage. Not only have you levied a personal insult, but you're also making a claim that the pattern is recurring, which means you're engaging in more than one battle at a time.

Rather than utilizing ad hominem in our vocabulary, I strive to redirect the emotional energy of these moments into more helpful phrases with myself and our children. This means attacking undesired behavior with precision, rather than assaulting the individual and their character. Instead of leveling the accusation to another human being that "you're an idiot," try to stay focused on what you believe to be the issue at hand: "It wasn't smart to drive 30 mph over the speed limit." While the distinction here is subtle, the difference of adopting this habit is significant. This instruction is similar to avoiding negative self-talk, but within the context of how we talk to or about others. Name-calling ends any semblance of a real conversation; there's not much left to say in response to "You're an idiot" except to get defensive, have your feelings hurt, or fire back with your own personal insult. Humans naturally don't take personal, character-defining accusations very lightly. Our prefrontal cortex, the part of the brain that processes real-time information, basically shuts down and we go into our more animalistic fight or flight response mode. On the other hand, humans have a unique capacity for non-defensive reflection when we receive feedback that is directed at our actions or temporary behavior. In other words, it's much easier to agree with or at least be inquisitive upon hearing, "That was a dumb thing you just did," than it is to acknowledge, "You're so dumb." Both the person sharing the feedback and the person receiving the feedback now have an opportunity to engage in a healthy and productive discussion where the unsavory action is the topic rather than having a more emotionally charged defensive conversation.

Aspire to rid your family's vocab of name-calling across the board. Even when joking around or attempting to be playful, just decide that it's neither funny nor helpful. I've gotten to the point where hearing a personal attack is simply not tolerated. I want to be clear that this isn't about being passive or failing to confront uncomfortable situations at all. I have no problem with confrontation and I encourage it when it's necessary. My kids are not shy about discussing uncomfortable topics or addressing elephants in the room. If someone is BEING a jerk, it is okay to tactfully let them know they are BEING a jerk without calling them a jerk. Once you master this conversational tactic and enforce this simple key in your home, you and your family will find greater success in diffusing conflict and counterintuitively find more confidence when confronting situations that require bold leadership. It's a game changer.

This predictably goes back to the golden rule. This is how I want others to deal with me in moments where I'm falling short of their expectations—tell me directly that I've said or done something specific that you dislike and why so we can have a mature conversation about it and work toward a resolution. If you come at me with a personal insult that labels me some petty schoolyard name, you can expect a much different reaction. I'm not going to be offended if you call me an asshat or whatever, but I am going to relentlessly defend my character. The difference here is literally a matter of offense (being offended) versus defense (defending your character).

No Offense

It seems like people are more sensitive these days than what was commonplace for millennials like me growing up. And even millennials, now as adults, seem much more sensitive than previous generations. In our modern world, we are increasingly pressured into walking on eggshells to avoid offending people for whatever issue they have developed a sensitivity to in any given context. Gender, race, sexuality, age, disabilities, marital status, job status, pronouns, class, immigration status, and even vaccination status have become cultural flashpoints that can get you canceled (whatever that even means). Humans have really turned caring about what people think into worrying about what people think a little too much. I have a loose personal policy that basically makes me immune to being offended. The policy is: don't get offended. Look, I'm a simple man. Being offended is an emotion that I've decided isn't worth my time or energy. If you think about it, allowing yourself to be offended is allowing others to impose a feeling on you that you didn't sign up for. This is different from being hurt or angry. Being offended isn't so much an emotion as it is a burden that someone is trying to place on your shoulders. I've just decided to say no thanks to that burden. It works great. My favorite is when people start a sentence with, "No offense, but...," because you know whatever comes out of their mouth next is likely going to be at least mildly offensive by most standards. But just as before, just because something may be *offensive* doesn't require you to be *offended*. Choosing to be offended is up to the person on the receiving end.

I say all of that to qualify the No Name-Calling rule. The idea isn't coming from a place of being highly sensitive as commanded by the prevailing culture. Rather, it is a vocabulary weapon to be utilized and taught to children, almost like a form of intellectual martial arts. Name-calling is weak. Measured confrontation with precise language is more powerful. Personally, I think it's unfortunate that the pendulum is beginning to swing so far in the other direction where we're now seeing slurs like "r*tard" and "f*g" make somewhat of a comeback, especially on X/Twitter. It's not surprising that people are lashing out against the overbearing tone policing that has become commonplace. But it is a bit unfortunate, especially when observed in the up-and-coming generations. You will not be missing out on anything by deciding to be someone who doesn't name-call others. In fact, I believe you will find more richness in your conversations and be a more effective parent by putting this key into practice.

If You Want to Make the World a Better Place

As we wrap up this section, we return full circle to The King of Pop's infamous lyrics. We've explored the idea of Showing

Up by utilizing the APPIE acronym, Self-Awareness and the importance of reflecting on "What's in Your Hand," Self-Talk and the imperative to "Worry about yourself," and finally the MMA of vocabulary: We don't Name-Call or get offended. Deep down, most humans aspire or once aspired to make a difference in the world to the extent allowed by their own vision, ambitions, and capabilities. Perhaps some have given up and fallen into nihilism or hopelessness. But for those of us who still have a flicker of passion to see the world change for the better, if not for our own sake, than certainly for the sake of our children, the cliche of starting with yourself bears deep truth. **93% of Sound Parenting is working on yourself and becoming a better human.** The other 7% is teaching your kids about Bitcoin. You can't fact-check this stat because I made it up, but I'm almost certain it's accurate.

Even the most ambitious dreamers among us recognize that changing the world takes time. Lots and lots of time. It also takes a lot of self-reliant, well-spoken, and mature people. Lots and lots of people. So, while I believe the "starting with the man in the mirror" cliche bears much truth, I also believe that the imperative for parents carries the added responsibility of modeling, guiding, and equipping your children with the tools to do likewise. In other words, don't just start with the man in the mirror and ask him to change his ways. Continue with your offspring by helping them check themselves and encouraging them to follow your lead. This is how we, the dreamers and believers in a better world, ultimately win. But we're just getting warmed up!

Section 1 Next Steps

- Recall the past 48 hours and every interaction you've had with your children. Give yourself a rating from 1-10 on how present you were: 1 being "YouTube did most of the parenting" and 10 being "phone was off, built a LEGO mansion." Do this again in a week and see if you can get that number to go up.
- Call a family meeting. Discuss the key principles of "Watch Your Self-Talk" and "We Don't Name-Call." Set the expectation that name-calling will not be tolerated, even if "joking," and negative self-talk will be gently corrected. Reconvene after a week to check in on your family's progress and gather feedback for making these habits stick.
- Look at your calendar for the next week. Select at least one upcoming event to intentionally practice Showing Up. Recall the APPIE acronym and write a brief plan for how you will implement these steps. Try this in various environments, and when you feel comfortable walk your kids through the same exercise.

SECTION 2
Let's Talk About Words, Baby

By now you may have picked up on a common theme: vocabulary. Hard to believe I have more to say about this topic, but alas, welcome to Section 2: Let's Talk About Words, Baby. Yes, this will include all the good things, and the bad things, that may be.

If you are parenting Gen Z kids, you might have noticed a propensity to shorten the words they use in their interactions. Perhaps this phenomenon is a byproduct of the proliferation of text messaging, social media, and non-verbal forms of communication taking over our culture. But regardless of the cause of this seemingly recent development, the side effects are alarming.

Fine tuning your language and guiding your children to prioritize thoughtfulness with the words they use requires discipline. This again seems especially true for those of us raising Gen Z kids who essentially have their own dictionary of new terms. Of course every generation throughout history is distinguished at least in part by the slang terms they invented and claimed as their own. These words often come and go like fashion trends and even change meaning as their originators age out. But what's unique about Gen Z is the speed at which they can develop and deploy their creative lingo, thanks to the ubiquity and acceleration of new technology.

In this section we'll examine some vocabulary landmines and how to best avoid them, and introduce a few ways that a nuanced approach to language can improve the quality of your communication with your child. By prioritizing intentional and effective use of our words, we continue on our quest toward practicing Sound Parenting.

CHAPTER 7
USE YOUR WORDS

A baby's first words are among the most special moments in the life of a new parent. Whether it's hearing your young offspring utter "mama," "dada," or "poopoo" for the first time, it is a memory that parents cherish as a critical milestone. Babies obviously don't emerge from the womb and start talking. This is for the simple reason that language is a human innovation that must be taught—first through expression and then learned through comprehension. After the novelty of the first few words wears off, one of the next most potent observations for a young parent is hearing their kids begin parroting something they said, which can catch you off guard depending on what it is they are repeating.

Perhaps this is a good time to acknowledge that I don't know anyone, my wife and I included, who were fully prepared to become parents. Sure, in those early days we read the books, sought mentorship, and leaned into our own experiences to help us along the way. Nevertheless, there are some aspects of parenting that may seem obvious in hindsight, but until you experience them for yourself, you realize how much you have to learn. This is still true even as our kids enter their teenage years. Intentionality when it comes to teaching your kids about the words they use is one way I hope to contribute to helping parents become a little more prepared on their journey. It's mostly a common sense, matter-of-fact, "I wish someone would have told me that" kind of a thing that I believe has been largely neglected among many parents at large. For Team Mekhail, the mantra "Use Your Words" was one of the earliest ones I recall implementing, even before the kids started forming verbal sentences.

SIGN YOUR MANNERS

Please. Thank You. More. Stop. All done. If you are in the pre-verbal stage of parenting, commit to learning these five words using sign language and thank me later. I'm not going to try to teach you the motions here, but I bet Google or maybe ChatGPT can help with that part. I still remember the signs for these five words and I don't exactly use sign language regularly, so they must have left an impression. Danielle has actually continued to use the sign for "Stop" even as the kids became older. No one wants to be the parent yelling at their kid from across the room. Learning to communicate with older kids in a way that doesn't require embarrassing them is also a helpful tip. I can still picture my infant children, struggling to verbalize what they wanted or needed, and how critical teaching them sign language was in those stages of their development. Not only was it important from the standpoint of establishing basic manners at an early age, but it was also the precursor to the "Use Your Words" mantra which is still relevant for us to this day.

If you polled any random group of parents about the most desired trait they wished to instill in their children, I imagine "being well-mannered" would be near the top of the list. It's such an obvious, common sense, universal aspect of raising children that it's almost not worth making a case for why it is important. But that is exactly what we're going to do because if you've scrolled TikTok lately, it seems many parents are choosing to neglect this basic imperative.

Manners are not only foundational to almost every other aspect of parenting, but they are also one of the earliest opportunities for parents to teach kids *how to learn* and to *practice how to teach.*

SAY YOUR NAME, SAY YOUR NAME

Foundational to manners is self-respect and self-awareness. This starts by knowing your own name and not being afraid to use it. Adults know that in social situations, when you are meeting a new person for the first time, the proper protocol is to smile, extend your right hand, look them in the eye, and say something to the effect of, "Hi, my name is Xavier, nice to meet you." Most dads will emphasize the importance of a firm handshake as well (which is great), but the key here is that you actually have to teach your kids to do this proactively and not expect them to simply know this is the expected drill. I cannot tell you how many times people have been impressed with Kingston and Saxyn just for the simple fact that they know how to introduce themselves, which is why I want to spell it out as an item on your parental to-do list. Each aspect is important: Smile. Eye-Contact. Handshake. Say your name. Nice to meet you. Say it with confidence and with a loud enough voice that is appropriate for the setting.

Introductions can be awkward, even for adults, so imagine how much more intimidating it is for children. But if they can master this easy skill early in life, they will once again be well-equipped as they continue to grow and mature. What follows is probably even more important: hearing the response and learning the other person's name. Bonus points if they repeat it back like, "Jason? Nice to meet you, Jason." This is also a great way to retain the person's name so you don't immediately forget it. We all know that half the time we're too caught up thinking about ourselves when making an intro that we forget to actually listen to what the other person says, so getting in the habit of repeating the name back every time helps ensure you're attentive all the way through. Look, I know this is very basic stuff, but the point here again is that you actually have to teach your kids how to do these basic things step by step.

Once the basics of introductions are understood, the intimidation factor begins to fade. You will find that your children are more comfortable around adults when they have the ability to naturally break the ice. This requires practice and encouragement, but you can't always bail them out or do it for them. If you're not already in the habit of introducing your kids when they are with you, then it's on you to help facilitate these interactions. There is nothing worse than being the person awkwardly standing there while two people carry on a conversation and you haven't been introduced. This happens A LOT to non-adults, which is a tragedy in my humble opinion. Be proud and excited to introduce your kids and offer them the opportunity to practice their social skills literally any time they are with you. Otherwise, what are they doing there? It's not hard to ask, "Jason, have you met my son?" and then let young Jefferson take it from there (by the way, you should do this with adults too—don't be that guy that leaves their friend hanging in the lurch while you're talking to all your buddies at a party). Once again, you are a mirror. As your kids observe you practicing these social skills, they will follow suit, and you are more confidently able to teach the skills that you yourself have mastered. We're finding this life hack to be especially helpful as our kids enter their early teenage years and have more and more friends coming around. They've naturally learned that anytime a new child comes to our home, the first thing they do is introduce them to us. It's a thing of beauty to be able to watch the things you've taught your kids come full circle this way as they begin to model and teach it to others with their own behavior.

SAY WHAT YOU MEAN, MEAN WHAT YOU SAY

When we remind our kids to "Use Your Words," we're encouraging them to be a whole entire human being who demands respect. They cannot always look to Mom and Dad to bail them out or interpret their wants and needs. The earlier they learn to fend for themselves, the better. As the saying goes, "Closed mouths don't get fed!" We took this very literally as early as the kids could talk by insisting that they order their own food at restaurants. Another great training ground to allow your children to practice assertiveness, confidence, and vocabulary. In the early going of learning how to order food from a restaurant, there will be moments of discomfort and you might get unlucky with an impatient server who just wants to get the order and move on to the next table. You may even find yourself being the impatient one. But the struggle is part of the journey, and most of the time servers are happy to oblige when they see that you are in the middle of a teaching moment. Use phrases like, "Tell them, not me," as your kids fumble through the uncertainty of having to look another adult in the eye and make a request. Encourage them to "speak up" and answer all the questions. Some kids will pick this up right away and others will require more practice, but the point is they must be given the opportunity, rather than having you order for them until they are 18.

Teaching your kids to Use Their Words is a formative skill that spans many aspects of Sound Parenting. Not only does it help instill confidence, but it also teaches assertiveness and helps quell self-doubt. Remember the goal is to raise resilient, self-reliant kids who will thrive in the real world without you needing to constantly look over their shoulder. This fundamental skill isn't picked up overnight and it doesn't happen by accident. It requires thoughtfulness on the part of the parent to ensure that ample opportunities are given to practice in real time so that these skills can be further honed. We like to remind our kids to "Say what you mean and mean what you say." Said differently: don't be lazy with your words.

CHAPTER 8
LIMIT ABSOLUTES

An "absolute" is a declarative word or phrase which leaves no room for exceptions. This includes words like "everyone," "always," and "never." A long-standing Team Mekhail rule is to avoid and interrogate the use of absolutes. The primary reason for this rule is to encourage the use of more precise language and discourage lazy or inaccurate accusations and declarations. Absolutes also have a way of shutting down conversation and creating unhelpful labels which can easily become wrapped up in identity, similar to what we discussed in the "No Name-Calling" chapter.

When you say to someone, "You are ALWAYS so loud!" you have levied an accusation which offers very little room for a mature or productive rebuttal. The only options they're left with are to either deny the accusation outright or accept the label as reality and cope with this trait as an inherent part of their personality. This is especially true when a parent speaks in negative and condemning absolute statements to a young child who is still wrestling with and forming their actual identity. In this stage of life, they are looking to sources of authority to help define who they are and what they are about. Parents must be extra cautious when utilizing absolute language in their parenting, especially when the context involves heightened emotion. I'm not a psychologist, but I imagine this is how trauma begins to set in.

Avoiding or limiting absolutes can be a difficult exercise in our modern world because of how deeply ingrained it is as a linguistic habit for English speakers. Just for fun, try not to use absolutes for an entire day and see how it goes. Now that I've pointed it out, you will notice its prominent place in our everyday vocabulary and how powerful it can be to make this minor modification.

We've already established the importance of teaching children to Use Their Words, so it's critical to closely follow-up that teaching by helping them learn to properly wield the essential tools of vocabulary. I believe that helping them become mindful of their use of absolutes challenges them to actively think about the words they are using and avoid being lazy with the words they throw around. A lot of emotion is typically packed into delivering an absolute statement, so this mental checkpoint serves as a conversational speed bump and a real-time fact checker. Instead of, "You are ALWAYS so loud!" a more helpful and revealing phrase is required like, "Can you please keep it down?" or in the infamous words of Taylor Swift, "You're being too loud!"

I Know & I Don't Know

By encouraging kids to choose their words more carefully, new habits begin to form that stretch their intellectual capacity. No more lazy language. If you say to me, "everyone has Instagram," you can expect me to ask, "Who is everyone?" This is an invitation to greater specificity. Say what you mean, mean what you say—and be prepared to defend every word you use because words are powerful.

Two of my least favorite phrases are the absolute assertions "I know" and "I don't know." I dislike them for obvious reasons. They're indolent, throw-away phrases that rarely carry the meaning they are intended to communicate. When one of my kids says "I know" in response to something I've just said, chances are they in fact do not know. Otherwise, I wouldn't have needed to tell them whatever it was I just got done telling them. Sound parenting requires you to challenge the use of such phrases consistently. Every. Time. For younger children, the use of, "I know" can often be a dismissive if not disrespectful retort to your instructions. This is a good time to gently correct them with, "Yes, mom," which is often a more accurate and appropriate response. On the other hand, "I don't know" is equally problematic. If I just asked you a question, and the best response you can come up with is "I don't know," that typically means you weren't listening, are uninterested, or (again) simply being too lazy to engage in an intellectual exchange. Quality conversation requires effort and alertness. If I catch you flat-footed and you hit me with an "I don't know," you better believe there will be a follow-up question. With my kids, that might be a simple "try again," or in extreme cases, rephrasing or repeating what I just said until I am able to extract a more worthwhile response. If you think about it, both phrases are basically synonyms of "whatever," which, when it comes to parenting, is often the height of disrespect. **I would encourage parents to be vigilant when addressing the lazy vocabulary siblings "I know" and "I don't know" and confront them with zeal so they do not become habitual staples of your children's vocabulary.**

SOME RESTRICTIONS APPLY

Yes, I understand that sometimes when someone says, "I know," they do in fact know. And I acknowledge that every now and then, when an "I don't know" is uttered, the person actually doesn't know. This is where discernment and best judgment is required. Perhaps your instructions are confusing and you need to clarify what you're saying to elicit a more meaningful response. But in both cases this is the exception to the rule.

The paradox with the rule of absolutes is that it can SOMETIMES feel stifling and ironically serve as an absolute unto itself. If I said, "Don't EVER use absolutes," well, that would be an absolute, and I would be a hypocrite. There are times in life where absolutes are simply true. If there is a unanimous vote to eat Mexican food for dinner, then it's just true that "everyone" wants to eat Mexican food for dinner. So, the point is simply to become aware of absolutes being used in everyday language as a method of identifying and confronting conversational apathy.

As you become more aware of how absolutes are utilized and begin to intentionally limit them in your everyday vocabulary, you will promote healthier and more mature conversations. This tactic is especially useful during heated arguments and is typically the best training ground for this Sound Parenting technique. The goal isn't to be pedantic but to foster more precision and challenge unfounded exaggeration.

Clear Over Cute

In my marketing days, one of my favorite rules of thumb was "Clear over Cute" and I believe it's a relevant anecdote here as well. The idea is that anytime you're attempting to communicate a message, it can be easy to get caught up in making it look nice or appear pretty while neglecting to effectively deliver whatever it is that you're trying to say. We live near a unique little market that features appealing architecture and sells phenomenal products. The problem is it's called Air Guitar. When we first moved to the area, we would drive by it and literally have no idea what it was they were selling or if they were even selling anything. What does "Air Guitar" even mean? Was it a gas station? We didn't see any pumps. Perhaps they sell instruments? That's a weird spot for an instrument store. It wasn't until we went into the store to check it out that we understood it was a boutique market where I also inadvertently discovered some of my favorite sushi in town (if Whole Foods made a mini-mart, it would be Air Guitar).

Over time they must have received similar feedback from many customers about their confusing, unclear signage, because they began adding supplemental signage transitioning away from *cute* and toward *clear*. First, they added a sign that said, "Super Cool Food Store." Okay, that's better, but still not quite getting the point across. Eventually, they added several large-font signs simply stating what they sold "BEER," "SUSHI," "ICE CREAM," and so on. Boom, now we're talking!

This example highlights the importance of precision in language and the need to be explicit in our communication if we wish to get our message across. That is the essence of limiting absolutes: to cut to the chase and avoid just trying to sound good. It's easy to tell your child they NEVER take the trash out when you ask them, but it requires much more thoughtfulness to say, "I've noticed you've neglected to take out the garbage for the third week in a row. How can we get you back on track so that you don't need repeated reminders?"

By practicing the habit of avoiding absolutes, we begin to expand our vocabulary. We hold ourselves and our children to a higher standard when it comes to language and we demand precision in communication. The accumulation of all these skills ultimately serves our desired end of Sound Parenting, which once again is developing quality character both in ourselves and our children. We become more grounded, confident, and thoughtful in every interaction. Avoiding absolutes is a skill that requires both critical thinking and attentiveness. These can be habits that are solidly engrained and not easily movable. Attempt to move them anyway. I believe that if more people watched the way they use absolutes, we could improve the quality of common discourse considerably. Perhaps we could slowly even begin to live in a slightly kinder society.

CHAPTER 9
KIND > NICE

It would be impossible to cover all the linguistic anecdotes that I believe are essential to Sound Parenting, so we're going to hit the ones that we've found to be the most helpful in raising our own kids. "Kind over nice" has become a handy reminder that allows us to make a key distinction in one of the English language's most commonly used and (in my opinion) most misunderstood words: "nice." How many times have you said something like, "Oh, he's SO NICE!" but low-key second-guessed the accuracy of that statement deep down in your soul immediately after saying it? Chances are high that if you are meaning to be genuinely complimentary, you will dig up a more robust, meaningful adjective. The word nice is overused to describe just about anything remotely positive about a person, interaction, or gesture. Don't get me wrong—I do not think "nice" is necessarily bad—it's often just naively innocent in its usage. That said, I do believe there is a level of discernment one should apply when evaluating anything labeled as "nice." Consider how the word is also used to express simple sarcasm or the subtle if not ironic truth behind the phrase "Nice guys finish last." What is it about this word that warrants further exploration?

In reality what we often describe as nice could just as easily mean fake or inauthentic. Most people are nice. Pleasantries are nice. **Being nice is not hard; it's the bare minimum standard for a human to achieve common decency.** You don't have to know someone in order to be nice to them. Smiling at a stranger is nice. Talking about the weather is nice. Oh, that person is always so nice when we talk. Again, it's usually not bad. But it is almost as if the word has experienced some sort of vocabulary inflation, having been used so ubiquitously as to cheapen its intended meaning. Isn't that nice?

I've slow-played this a bit because now I'm going in for the kill. I'd like to address how frequently the word nice becomes misleading to the point of being nefarious. Sometimes people with an agenda are nice. While this is also a helpful tool for adults, the importance of teaching your children this distinction helps train them to remain on high alert and become more vigilant in detecting bullshit. People who have malicious intentions are nice on the surface. People who intend to manipulate typically appear nice before revealing their hidden motivations. Used car salesmen are nice. Kidnappers offering you candy are nice. You get the picture (for the record, just to clarify, I'm in no way saying used car salesmen are in the same category of kidnappers. Actually, the used car salesman stereotype isn't very nice if I'm being perfectly honest. Most of them are just out here trying to sell a car and make a living). Anyways, the key is to exercise a level of shrewdness when handling this word. The lesson is to practice not being overly impressed with someone being nice or immediately feeling obligated in response to a nice gesture. Nice is basic at best, insincere at worst.

Niceness in Psychology

One of my favorite books, Robert Cialadini's *Influence: The Psychology of Persuasion*, explores six primary ways that human decision-making works, almost at a subconscious level. The six principles of influence are reciprocity, scarcity, authority, commitment and consistency, liking, and social proof. Without going too far down this rabbit hole, I want to highlight that two of these principles lean into some level of "niceness" in order to accomplish their desired goal of persuasion: reciprocity and liking.

The principle of reciprocity states that people are obliged to give back to others the form of a behavior, gift, or service that they have received first. As an example, if a friend invites you to their birthday party, there's an underlying sense of obligation for you to invite them to a future party you are hosting. More relevant to our purposes: if a boyfriend pays for dinner, you might say, "Oh, that was nice," when in reality there is an unspoken expectation (or not-so-subtle pressure) to reciprocate that gesture with a sexual favor. I realize that just escalated quickly, but this bluntness is essential to the point I'm making and the reason for vigilance when it comes to approaching this linguistic trap. You might say, "What a cynical way to view the world"—unless of course you're a father with daughters (and in that case you are likely busting out your highlighter). But let's also keep in mind that raising boys to understand this nuanced skill is just as important. In order for these situations to be avoided, it starts with young men raising their level of awareness as to how they may unintentionally create unspoken expectations with someone's daughter. This doesn't mean discouraging young men from buying dinner for their date for fear of creating a false expectation. Please hear that. But growing in this aspect of situational awareness ensures the dynamics that are at play are fully understood, which is helpful knowledge to be equipped with for everyone involved. It's perfectly acceptable to accept the gesture for what it is without falling into this psychological dilemma to satisfy the innate human response of reciprocity. I'm not suggesting you question the motives behind every nice gesture or every birthday party invitation you receive from now on, but I am stressing the importance of discernment and awareness in order to avoid being taken advantage of and helping your kids understand the same. Guys should be able to pay for dates without needing anything in return. Likewise, girls should enjoy their dates, paid for by their guys, without feeling the need to offer something in return. Even a second date!

The second relevant principle of influence as it relates to the psychology of persuasion is "liking." What is the liking principle? Simply put, we tend to like people who are similar to us in some way—people who offer us compliments and people who cooperate or seem to cooperate with us toward a shared goal. According to the liking principle, we are more likely to be persuaded by people we like and those we want to be like. Many salespeople are trained to begin every interaction with a prospective client by first offering them a compliment or a beverage for this very reason. Nothing earth-shattering here, but you can see how small the leap is from someone being perceived as "nice" to then liking that person as a result. It is obviously naive to think everyone who smiles at you has your best interest at heart or that every compliment you receive is sincere. The liking principle also helps illuminate much of the power behind peer pressure which again is useful for increasing awareness. By identifying and even anticipating these dynamics and how they play out in social situations, parents can be better equipped with simple tools for helping their children avoid common pitfalls, especially in young adults and teenagers. Not everyone you say is nice is your friend.

You Can't Fake Kind

The truth is niceness can be used as bait to what can ultimately turn into behavior that is otherwise "cruel" or "mean." People who gossip about you behind your back are often nice to your face. Students are nice in class with their peers, perhaps in an attempt to receive a better grade. Even toddlers, as innocent as they appear, aren't that nice. They seem nice by default usually because they have a parent looming behind them telling them to *be* nice. Not kind. Nice.

Ultimately, making this distinction is meant to return us back to the goal of understanding and helping develop strong character in our children. People of high character are of course genuinely nice, but they also grasp the level of superficiality that is tied up with mere niceness, and aspire to cultivate and demonstrate authentic *kindness* when appropriate. Not only that, but teaching your children about pattern recognition can help with critical life decisions, including identifying true friends and avoiding situations where they can end up getting wounded in some way, shape, or form. And you thought this was a simple vocabulary lesson!

Once we graduate from mere niceness, we can begin to appreciate the depth and power of the word "kind" while expanding the prowess of our vocabulary tool belt. I'm not claiming that I just taught you a new word, and I realize the word "kind" is also a popular one. But it's almost been overshadowed by nice for too long. It is time we bring "kind" out of the shadows and use it to make these critical distinctions. The truth is, you can't fake kindness the same way you can fake niceness. It takes only a little more effort to describe someone or something as kind, but you'll find that this effort is usually made gladly when the distinction seems necessary. When you experience true, genuine kindness, it causes you to pause and ensure it is appropriately acknowledged. This is when the word "nice" simply falls short.

If this is true and these behaviors are somewhat ingrained (as evidenced by the way we respond), why not exercise a dash of intentionality and attempt to be more mindful in how we use these words? Say what you mean and mean what you say. If something is kind, call it kind. And most of all, if you don't know how to describe something, it's perfectly okay to not describe it at all.

CHAPTER 10
DON'T USE WORDS YOU CAN'T DEFINE

All words matter. Having a high regard and profound respect for the words that we use is a critical aspect of effective parenting. An approach that is all too common is the predictable categorization of vocabulary into binary categories of "good/acceptable" and "bad/curse" words. The goal with this dubious parenting tactic seems to be aimed at ensuring your kids don't drop an F-bomb in front of Grandma. While this may be a noble end, I question the effectiveness of the means to ensure Grandma's ears are protected. This next key is one of my favorites. I consider it something of a parenting hack that unlocks a cheat code, especially with very young children who are just learning how to talk, but also as they progress, are exposed to outside influences, and start learning new and exciting words they're eager to share. It starts by establishing a foundational house rule that states "don't use words you can't define." From there, anytime you hear one of your kids use a questionable word or phrase, the next step is to simply ask, "Hey Alfred, what does [word in question] mean?" The ensuing conversation then ranges from hilarious to enlightening and everything in between.

The process of enforcing this house rule is as straightforward as you might imagine. Kid says a questionable word, the parent asks, "Do you know what that word means?" and nine times out of ten you will find that they have no idea. They will often offer a sheepish "no" in which case all that's left to do is remind them of the house rule. Other times they might say "yes" followed by a hilariously incorrect definition. In both cases, a learning opportunity has been created. Depending on the context, the age of the child, and the word or phrase in question, it can be a great time to share the sometimes uncomfortable definition of the word they just used. Sometimes this is the end of the discussion and frankly it's okay to move on depending on the context. It may not be time to ensure your 5-year-old gets the full download on what an "asshat" is as long as you've successfully nipped it in the bud.

However, most of the time the realization and admission that they don't know what a particular word means produces childlike curiosity, which can lead to fascinating discussions. I'll let you decide when it makes the most sense to provide these lessons as appropriate, but I will say that we've found that leaning into the discomfort is a phenomenal teacher. It's important not to blush or embarrass them in these situations. If it's a particularly strong word, it's okay to be serious as you're helping them understand the meaning and reinforcing the reason for the house rule. "This is why we don't use words that we can't define because we end up saying things we don't understand and don't mean." Again, these can be delicate moments, so handle them with care. It can also unexpectedly prompt follow-up questions about other words now that you've demonstrated you're open to dialogue. I still remember an entire conversation at dinner that started with one of the kids saying a penis euphemism which I won't repeat here. After a similar exchange to what I described above, both kids proceeded to ask about other words, and we obliged. By the end, we had what I believe was a healthier version of the classic "birds and the bees" conversation, without it feeling forced and with our kids leading the question asking.

The great thing about this rule is its versatility. Even in the off chance the child knows exactly what the word means, you've still created a teaching moment by asking them to define it. Kingston recently used a word at dinner: we made him define it and he ended up knowing exactly what it meant. Regardless, no child wants to sit there and provide the dictionary definition of vulgar slang words to their mother and father. By forcing the issue through the means of defining the words being used, you are creating dialogue and attacking the root of the issue, rather than positioning yourself as the immediate arbiter of "good versus bad" words. In other words, rather than dismissively passing judgment and selectively enforcing vague language boundaries, you allow the occasional discomfort of confronting an unsavory word and allowing that felt discomfort to serve as a lesson unto itself as to why the word may be inappropriate. Hopefully you can see how this is a more helpful approach than, "Hey! Don't say that—that's a bad word!" As your kids continue to grow and as the complexity of words in question increases, you may realize that the "list of banned words" approach will become an utter cluster fork.

STOP LYING

The underlying issue with using words you can't define is you are basically telling a lie. This may sound like a stretch, but hear me out. If the purpose of language is to communicate thoughts, feelings, or emotions, it stands to reason that you must first understand what you are saying before you can make an honest expression. Obviously, there is an element of intent required for it to truly constitute a lie, but when we are talking about kids mindlessly repeating words they heard on YouTube or at school, one could argue that the act of using that word is a dishonest expression. While I don't recommend making this specific point to your kids as a parenting tactic in these moments, I do think it's a helpful thought experiment to drive home the point that words are powerful and must be treated with care. The most honest use of words is in the expression of language that is well understood.

On the other hand, if this pattern of behavior is frequently repeated, it may be a red flag, rooted in some other form of dishonesty. Dealing with lying, even when it comes to small fibs, is among the greatest challenges a parent will face. It goes without saying that a fundamental aspect of Sound Parenting is a high regard for the truth, even if it's uncomfortable or inconvenient. We take this to the extreme, and I'd encourage you to do the same. If you are at a water park that sells discounted tickets for children eight and under, and your child is nine, consider if paying the extra $4.50 is worth it while your child is observing how much value you place on your integrity. It's difficult to enforce a high standard for the truth if you're making these minor compromises, especially under the watchful and ever-observant eyes of your young ones.

Do Not Love Half Lovers

My love for words made this a fun section to write and hopefully a helpful one to read. I want to close it out by reiterating some of the ground we've covered. It starts with encouraging your kids to Use Their Words. Communication is the bedrock of any healthy relationship, including your relationship with your kids. If they aren't talking to you from an early age and you're not engaging them with curiosity and intrigue, now would be a great time to correct this pattern. Frankly, this isn't one of those things that gets better with time. Help them learn assertiveness by encouraging them to speak up, order at restaurants, and introduce themselves in social situations. Emphasize the importance of the words they use by highlighting the need to Say What They Mean and Mean What They Say. Khalil Gibran puts this beautifully in his incredible poem, "Do Not Love Half Lovers," when he says:

If you choose silence, then be silent

When you speak, do so until you are finished

Do not silence yourself to say something

And do not speak to be silent

If you accept, then express it bluntly

Do not mask it

If you refuse then be clear about it

for an ambiguous refusal is but a weak acceptance....

In other words, show up and say it with your whole being! As you're leaning into your aspiration to be more expressive and varied with your vocabulary, remember to pay attention to absolutes and limit them as appropriate. Interrogate every "I know" and every "I don't know" with vigor and challenge your children to exercise critical thinking when they might prefer to prematurely end a discussion. These are the moments where Sound Parenting actually takes place. In these margins that are often overlooked and glossed over during our hurried lives. Teach your children to make a distinction between niceness and kindness and help them discern situations where they are being flattered or potentially being taken advantage of.

Aspire for kindness as a cornerstone trait for the overall character you are looking to instill in your child. And finally, confront every questionable word out of your child's mouth if there is any question that they do not know the definition of the word they are saying. I believe that if you implement the keys discussed in this section, you will unlock some incredible conversations with your kids while learning more about them and yourself in the process. But just like every key in this book, it will require practice, clarity, and consistency if you want it to stick. These don't set in as habits overnight. You will have to first determine whether you agree that they will be helpful and then commit to communicating and enforcing them in your home.

Section 2 Next Steps

- If your kids are new to the world, commit to learning these five words/phrases in sign language: Please. Thank You. More. Stop. All done. Teach them to your kids and utilize them as often as appropriate.
- Call a family meeting. This time, teach your children the keys to Limiting Absolutes, establish your expectation that "I Know & I Don't Know" will be interrogated moving forward, and describe the differences between the words "Kind & Nice."
- If you have a "swear jar," replace it with a "Words You Can't Define" jar or make one using a Bitcoin wallet QR code. Create a new house rule that if a member of the family (including you) is caught using a word they can't define, they have to put 500 sats into the jar.

SECTION 3
Keep the Change

What a time to be alive. No, seriously. Are you not entertained? Of course you are with 47 different streaming services, access to unlimited information in your pocket, and a continuous stream of real-world events that are on similar levels of drama to soap opera plot lines. There is no shortage of entertainment all around us. There is no such thing as a slow news day anymore. We are more connected than ever, yet increasingly finding new ways to detach, divide, and social distance. With this ever-changing reality serving as the backdrop of our efforts to effectively parent young ones, challenges abound.

This section explores the broad theme of our rapidly changing world and the parental imperative to embrace the newness around us. Technology is here to stay; it is not something we can simply ignore as parents. Teaching our kids how to responsibly interact with devices could be an entire book, but we'll focus on unpacking the lessons Danielle and I have learned with the Sound Parenting key "Ringers on, Phone

Is Charged." On the flip side of the section title's monetary double entendre, we'll reflect on the importance of instilling the value of hard work in your children from an early age and explore a few practical guides for achieving this parental goal.

To close out the section, we dive into the deep end with a look at one of the most significant changes unfolding in our world with the topic of Bitcoin. The reality of Bitcoin in my life and impact it's had on my parenting style is simply unavoidable. It felt disingenuous (even irresponsible) not to give it proper airtime. My conviction is that this generation of parents would do well to properly educate themselves on its importance and the significant role it plays within the context of rapidly changing paradigms. Regardless of your familiarity with the topic, we can all admit that the relevance of this topic has increased significantly in the past ten years, and it stands to reason that ten years from the time of this writing, when your children are much older, it will be impossible to ignore.

Let's get to work.

CHAPTER 11
RINGER'S ON, PHONE IS CHARGED

O n January 9th, 2007, everything changed. If you look up the word "auspicious" in the dictionary, you will find a photo of Steve Jobs standing on the MacWorld stage in San Francisco, preparing to leave his industrial mark on humanity by introducing the world to the iPhone. Six months later, on June 29th, the 1st generation iPhone was available for purchase and the rest, as they say, is history. But the rest is also the present. And ironically, the iPhone is the very thing that is responsible for so much *lack* of presence in our world today. Before this consequential keynote, we had no idea that the implications of this curious device would reverberate so profoundly. I would argue we're still trying to figure out what exactly we're dealing with. I often think about the subtlety of the Apple logo's ominous bite mark. I don't believe in coincidences, so I can't help but notice how eerily similar this infamous corporate symbol is to the imagery depicted in the Garden of Eden.

Now listen, I'm typing this on a MacBook Pro, my iPhone is fully charged, and I tend to judge people who send me green texts more than I judge Eve for her alleged sin against humanity. I'm speaking to you as a fellow indulger of the forbidden fruit. I also acknowledge that even with all its negatives, the advancement of technology and the subsequent innovation that has emerged since the iPhone can almost be described as miraculous. Just like the tree in the garden with its tempting fruit, the iPhone itself did not cause "the fall" of the world. But perhaps our ongoing decision to live off of its fruit is somewhat allegorical to our modern-day addiction to our iPhones and the unquenchable pursuit of more knowledge, more entertainment, and the subsequent result of more isolation and anxiety. As if these dynamics aren't difficult enough to navigate as an adult, the minefield of emergent technology becomes even more daunting when you throw a kid or two into the mix.

Parental Controls?

No matter what I say about the subject of technology and navigating this tricky aspect of 21st century parenting, people across the spectrum of opinions will have strong reactions. The only thing I can offer is my own experience. Danielle and I opted to get both of our kids' phones earlier than most parents. We made decisions based on our own unique circumstances with the information we had to work with at the time. Parents with young ones today are faced with a similar set of questions they too will have to navigate.

Kingston was born one year after the iPhone was released. We didn't exactly have a lot of time to develop a cohesive strategy for appropriate levels of screen time and parental controls weren't a thing quite yet. So we did what every loving parent would do in the situation: we made it up on the fly. We had to make several adjustments along the way. It was obviously pretty intuitive to recognize it was not healthy for a two year old to sit there and stare at a screen for hours on end. But at the same time, we understood that technology wasn't going anywhere—in fact, the rapid pace of technological advancement was clearly just heating up. There is a level of danger to both extremes of either letting Mickey Mouse Clubhouse serve as your babysitter or attempting to ban any and all interaction with devices altogether. You might be able to pull off one or the other strategy for a period of time with some semblance of short-term success. But guess what happens next? In the case of the former, your child becomes hopelessly addicted to the dopamine hit of The Hot Dog Song and in the case of the latter their curiosity as to what they're missing can turn into bitterness and defiance the moment the opportunity to interact with technology presents itself.

We cannot control our kids. We can only hope to positively influence them. This is true of infants' inconsolable crying and continues into their teens, where the innate human desire for independence really begins to crank up. Your children are sons of Adam and daughters of Eve. If that story was written today, instead of Eve handing Adam a bite of delicious fruit, she would be showing him the latest viral TikTok video and he'd laugh, and then they'd both keep mindlessly scrolling for 8 hours a day while slowly drifting apart. Your kids will fall many times throughout their lives. Sometimes it will hurt really bad and sadly, for the sake of your broken heart, there's very little you can do about it. One of the more instructive aspects of the Garden of Eden story is the depiction of God as a loving father, watching his children commit a costly mistake, despite his clear instructions attempting to spare them from significant pain. Regardless of your take on the Bible, the story still offers profound wisdom if we just take it at face value. It's almost like the lesson is about the predictability of human nature as revealed in the Creation account, along the lines of "if God can't control his kids, what makes you think you can control yours?" Perhaps tellingly, God doesn't seem interested in controlling them, which is also instructive. **Our role as parents is guidance and protection, not control and prevention.** The point is plain: resisting the powerful forces of nature and believing you can perfectly curate every environment your child will ever interact with is a short-sighted parental strategy. Aspire to protect them by establishing healthy boundaries, but avoid the mindset that you will always be able to prevent them from the eventuality of their own poor decisions.

MINDFUL MODERATION

A critical aspect of Sound Parenting is the ability to recognize and embrace reality for what it is. This requires you to continually adapt to multiple variables that are constantly changing. Your kids are getting older every day, and their curiosity about the world is only intensifying. Not only that, but all the fun, shiny, and tempting aspects of this world are accelerating while the ability to access them is becoming exponentially easier. Mindful moderation means having the ability to set reasonable boundaries while continually responding to what works and what does not work for your unique child and their particular temperament.

For us, that meant predictable daily screen time limits were allowed in the toddler years, but the content was strictly monitored. In addition to setting reasonable limitations on the allowable duration of screen time, we also devised various categories of content and created incentives for our children to prefer some forms of content versus others. Educational content was more favored than mindless "junk" content meant to deliver pure entertainment. Playing Minecraft was encouraged more than Madden. As the kids grew up, their screen time allocations became more detailed, with different times assigned to each category, which provided them with a level of autonomy within an established parental framework.

By embracing the reality of the existence of technology, we can better learn to wield them as the tools they are intended to be. In our experience, mindful moderation has been more effective than attempting to eliminate technology entirely, which I believe would have set us up for the eventuality of our children being exposed to their influence later in life, with no practice or roadmap for how they can interact with devices in a healthy way.

NO SCREENS AT THE TABLE

Eating a meal is sacred. There are few moments throughout the day that are to be intentionally set aside as distinct and unique from the other parts of the ordinary and mundane. Eating food is one such moment. There is simply no reason to have a phone or a screen out while you eat. Even leaving the television on. Perhaps one of the more simple and basic keys we enforce is a zero-tolerance policy for screens at the table. As commonsensical as it sounds, this one has a measurable impact on character and social development among children. Just look around a restaurant next time you're out and see how many humans are glued to their screens. In a world where it is easy to be consumed by the constant stream of notifications from social media, texts, and other apps competing for our attention, we need hard boundaries to unplug. Even for the adults. Food offers that practical excuse to abstain from our devices.

When we first implemented this rule, we all needed the occasional reminder to put our screens away. . Over time, the habit of focusing on food and present company during mealtimes has provided a healthy break from the over-stimulation that is now baked into our daily lives. Kingston mentioned recently that he was having dinner with some friends and found himself getting slightly irritated that he was often the only one not staring at his phone. This is the kind of "weird" we're going for (as if we're not already weird enough that we ensure family dinner a solid five nights a week).

We've had time to develop healthy habits, including the mantra "Ringers on, Phone is Charged" anytime we're going to be separated from our kids for one reason or another. To whom much is given, much is expected. If I'm going to provide you with the privilege of an iPhone, it will be within the confines of my rules. This means I am always able to get a hold of you, I can monitor your location as needed, and I can activate necessary protection at my discretion. In many ways, the decision to provide our kids with phones has served our own priorities as parents, including the underlying safety benefits that technology helps enable. We've had and continue to have many conversations with our kids about best practices, spanning interacting with friends and not sharing personal information to everything digital is permanent and don't take photos of people without their permission. We've also had to do the work of checking our own habits and ensuring we're not being hypocritical with the rules we enforce around technology.

Creating and practicing an intentional approach to technology in your home is hard work. But the avoidance of hard work must never be a determining factor in developing an effective parenting strategy. In fact, we must teach our kids the value of hard work with every chance we get and with the behavior that we model in our everyday decision-making.

CHAPTER 12
MONEY IS EARNED, NOTHING IS FREE

A s long as I can remember, the importance of hard work has been ingrained into the fabric of my being. My parents taught me this foundational principle not just with their words, but with the consistent example that they set in how they lived their lives and went about their business. Their story epitomizes the elusive quest for realizing the American Dream. When we first immigrated to the U.S. from Egypt in 1990, we didn't have much. But through hard work, determination, and pure grit, my parents fought their way to middle-class status in a few short years. The memory that sticks out the most from those early days was the time my dad worked three jobs, including the graveyard shift at Jack in the Box. My mom also worked two jobs while raising three kids. My parents taught me so much on this topic because it naturally oozed out of them from their own experience. If their goal was to create a better life for their family and set their children up to have more opportunities than they ever imagined possible, then

I can safely say mission accomplished. Not only am I proud of being raised to value the grind, but I am also motivated to instill the same values in my two children.

From a very early age, I was determined to make money. By the age of 12, I recall being frustrated at the limited opportunities that were available for kids to generate income. I attempted to satiate my hunger for work with the typical ideas other kids around my age pursued like lemonade stands and lawn mowing, but these attempts left me dissatisfied. Thankfully, the internet was starting to become a thing around this time, which was the very breakthrough I needed to truly tap into my entrepreneurial spirit. I attempted to start several new online ventures, often based on my hobbies and interests, before learning that just creating websites and sharing information wasn't a path to making money. By the time I was 13, I had finally gathered enough knowledge and learned from my many prior failures that I needed to zero in on a product that people would buy. Through much research and struggle, I landed on becoming a shoe retailer, and my first legit business, RareFootWear.com, was born. I do not know exactly why I landed on shoes as the thing I wanted to sell, but for whatever reason, I decided to dive in with both feet (pun alert!) and learn everything I could about the industry.

The business did okay to start, and I learned several additional lessons with each iteration. I got my big break in the shoe world when I connected with a new supplier in Hong Kong, which catapulted RareFootWear.com into becoming a relative success and a major asset to add to my resume. The lessons I learned at such a young age by applying the principles of hard work continue to serve me well in my ongoing career development and inform my outlook as a parent.

FAST FOOD TRIFECTA

My early success did not slow down my hustle mentality. Even while running my online shoe business, I still craved more opportunities. By the time I was 14, I was able to convince the store manager at the local Burger King to hire me as their youngest employee ever. Little did I know, Kingston would replicate this mini feat at the same age, landing a job at McDonalds and completing the three-generation Fast Food Trifecta that my dad started at Jack in the Box. I share these stories to establish a baseline for this chapter's key to Sound Parenting: Money Is Earned, Nothing Is Free. Both Danielle and I come from families that taught us we had to earn everything in this life and that nothing is handed to you. Naturally we've emphasized the same mentality with our kids every chance we get.

I can understand the propensity toward wanting to give your kids everything they ask for, no questions asked. I've seen this in families where one or both parents grew up somewhat poor, but in their own life managed to create wealth. In these scenarios, it makes sense to respond by attempting to ensure a child doesn't suffer the same fate and therefore utilize newfound wealth to spoil them with over-the-top gifts and a life of material abundance. But we know how this story ends. Kids that are not exposed to the struggle of earning often end up becoming entitled. They are conditioned to feel like they deserve the things they have because they never had to work for anything. This is obviously a perilous road to walk down, even with what is being communicated to children who are very young. Oftentimes the most loving thing you can do for your kids is refrain from granting their every desire and making all their dreams come true. That may sound harsh, especially if you're well off enough to afford granting every wish.

This is going to sound extreme to many readers, but I think the idea of giving your kids an allowance is a little ridiculous. I certainly never got an allowance, so perhaps my bias against the practice is showing. But there is some logic to my position. Allowance for what? Handing your kids free money every week for doing absolutely nothing is a scenario that is simply not replicated in the real world. What did they do to earn this free cash flow? If your answer is "chores," I'm going to address that specific topic later in this chapter. If your answer is "nothing," then my question is what are you teaching your child by handing them cash with no questions asked? I would venture to answer that question by saying you're teaching them to expect having money without the need to do anything. It may seem innocent and inconsequential, but I would challenge you to really interrogate the reasoning. It seems like it's one of those things that parents do because "everyone else does it." But doing things because they've always been done is simply not a good enough reason.

I understand that when kids reach a certain age, they begin finding themselves in situations where having a little spending money is very convenient. A little candy here, a movie with friends there—what's the big deal if I slide them a Jackson every week so they can go have fun? That's a slightly better question and an important point of clarification. I am not suggesting you don't treat your kids here and there or expect them to always pay for their own movie tickets. But I believe there is a significant difference between the practice of providing them with free cash flow in the form of a weekly allowance and subsidizing their one-off expenses within reason. In other words, buy them things with YOUR money when it's appropriate, but avoid establishing a dynamic where they have "their own money" that they did nothing to earn.

HIRE YOUR KIDS

The most common and perhaps strongest argument to refute my position on allowance is that kids are doing chores around the house and therefore earning the stipend. I get it, and this approach is certainly more valid than the allowance for doing nothing approach. However, there are some important nuances to explore with this popular approach. First, the correlation between emptying the dishwasher and receiving an allowance each week is not very strong. Even parents who carry out this model rigorously often fail to effectively communicate the connection between the task that is being completed and the money that is being provided as a result. It is often expected that the child will intuitively understand the dynamic because it seems like common sense. But even the language that is being used is problematic. The word "allowance" is overly permissive and suggests that they are receiving the funds as a result of simply existing in your home. The word "chore" is equally unhelpful. It is subtly communicating to the child that housework is an oppressive burden rather than a matter-of-fact necessity for a functioning household.

No one wants to do housework—not even the adults in the house. But even in the optimal execution of the "allowance for chores" paradigm, paying your kids for simple household tasks is also communicating that they don't have any real responsibilities as a member of the family. This is another way of creating a sense of entitlement and expectation that everything should be done for them. The allowance incentive robs them of the essential lesson of carrying their own weight. We believe that kids should have baseline responsibilities around the house and expect nothing in return besides a thank you. Keep in mind that you're already subsidizing their entire life. It is not unreasonable to expect them to contribute to small tasks like cleaning their room, unloading the dishwasher, taking out the trash, or cleaning up after dinner without any additional incentive being required.

That said, with these foundations clearly established, we've taken the approach of *hiring* our kids for jobs around the house that we might otherwise pay someone else to do or that we simply want to delegate in order to create the opportunity for them to earn. Deep cleaning the bathroom or detailing the car are examples of household jobs that require a bit more time and effort and are not necessarily essential to the day-to-day functioning of a household. The lines can get blurry, but the language and connection is always clear. If you clean the car, I will pay you X once the job has been completed to my satisfaction. Now they are investing real time and energy and you're genuinely getting your money's worth, which is not only a nice byproduct but also a valuable lesson for them to observe and feel good about. You can't fake this dynamic. Please do not pretend like the allowance to chore exchange is a realistic economic transaction. Kids can see through this hollow arrangement, and they also can grasp when they've actually completed a job and earned money by creating real value.

It's easy to misunderstand the subtlety of what I'm proposing, so if you do nothing else with this, perhaps consider adjusting your language from "chores and allowance" to "jobs and earning." If you put this key into practice, I believe you will be fostering an attitude in your kids that is more consistent with what they will experience in the real-world economy. It's never too early to learn about the critical dynamics of how money is earned—especially in our current world where economic incentives have been so misallocated and fake fiat jobs that provide no real value to society are celebrated and rewarded across a wide range of industries. This last piece has only become apparent to me since 2017 when I first got into Bitcoin (BTC). Ever since then, we've been paying our kids with satoshis for the jobs they are hired to complete, and teaching them valuable economic lessons along the way.

CHAPTER 13
The Future Is Orange

Bitcoin has become a significant influence in my life, and subsequently the life of my entire family. The more I have learned about Bitcoin, the more I've learned about human nature, economics, health, spirituality, sustainable communities, work and yes, family. All of these aspects of life impact the way I parent, and the further down the rabbit hole I travel, the more I've developed ways to bring my family along on this transformative journey.

Before we get too far into the practical ways that Bitcoin can serve your parental strategy, I want to explore a few of the basics of BTC for the uninitiated—starting with its association with the color orange. I recognize this can be a confusing topic and the following primer will fall woefully short of unpacking even the essentials about Bitcoin and why it matters. But if you're new to exploring this topic, you gotta start somewhere, so I will do my best to give you the highlights and hopefully build enough intrigue to encourage you to continue your own research. And by discussing Bitcoin within the context of parenting, I think fresh insights can emerge about its relevance beyond the mainstream talking points you may already be familiar with.

Digital Scarcity

Bitcoin is a new form of money. It was first launched by a pseudonymous developer named Satoshi Nakamoto back in 2010 and has since grown exponentially all around the world. In my opinion, its most important innovation is that for the first time ever, we have a form of currency which is perfectly, predictably, and verifiably scarce. There will only ever be 21 million bitcoin. That is the maximum supply. If you hear nothing else about the topic, hear this one simple fact and try to fully grasp its implications. Anyone with an internet connection can audit the supply of bitcoin at any time and can confirm that new bitcoins cannot be artificially produced and existing bitcoins cannot be duplicated. Compare this to the status quo of fiat currency which can be infinitely printed at the discretion and by the influence of a small group of powerful bankers, bureaucrats, and politicians.

Why is this important? If you look around, you will quickly notice that our economy is not only broken, but that it has been broken for a long time. One milestone that contributed to the acceleration of dollar debasement happened in 1971 when Nixon took the U.S. dollar off of the gold standard. Prior to this time, it was much more difficult to print money because it was required to be backed by a corresponding unit of gold. Most people do not consider the real world and even personal implications of money being printed without our approval, with very little effort, and with no corresponding value being created. This practice violates the very intention of money itself as a store of value, and monetary debasement of this sort is the hallmark of waning empires. This is where we find ourselves today in the United States—on the precipice of economic and societal calamity as we begin to reap what we've sown through irresponsible fiscal policy and unsustainable debt creation for over half a century. Bitcoin fixes this.

FIAT SLAVERY

Throughout human history, societies have attempted to resolve the limitations of various forms of money. Invariably, the same problems reoccur and the same lessons have to be relearned. Research the history of the Rai Stone, the fate of the Roman denarius, or more recently the Zimbabwean dollar. Each of these examples serve as a cautionary tale and reveal echoes of the U.S. dollar system. Despite these proven examples of doomed currencies, many people point to the digital nature of Bitcoin and the fact that you can't touch or hold a physical bitcoin as cause for concern. This is an understandable, but also a misguided and easily refutable objection. Even if Bitcoin didn't exist, the current trajectory of the U.S. dollar is a cashless future. Governments who wish to control, monitor, and tax every aspect of society want nothing more than to create a Central Bank Digital Currency (CBDC) and eliminate physical cash altogether.

This outcome should terrify us as parents who are concerned about the world our kids will inherit. It would quite literally result in a dystopian reality where governments can penalize your bank account if you participate in any form of wrong-think. They would be able to tax every transaction, from garage sales to babysitting, without you needing to file an annual tax return. They could make your money expire or limit who you could transact with for a variety of nefarious reasons. You get the picture. But Bitcoin is not controlled by any one individual, corporation, or central entity. It is fully distributed through a network of peers called "nodes" and is available to anyone in the world who wishes to opt-in to the open network. Anyone can audit the code that makes Bitcoin run, and anyone can see every transaction that has ever been and will ever be broadcast on the network.

The prospect of a government controlled CBDC alternative to Bitcoin isn't the only counterargument to the "lack of physicality" critique. The reality is that while you can't hold a physical unit of a bitcoin, you can observe the real-world, tangible evidence of its existence by visiting a Bitcoin mining operation near you. Without getting too far into the weeds of Bitcoin mining (which I find to be one of the most fascinating and exciting parts of the protocol), suffice to say that billions and billions of dollars are pouring into this unique and emergent new industry. You have to ask yourself why major energy companies like Shell are diverting resources to support the development of these physical outposts of bitcoin creation. This particular aspect of the Bitcoin world is accelerating at a breakneck pace, especially where energy is cheap and abundant. It is very much our modern-day version of the gold rush, except anyone with access to power can participate without having to travel to the shores of San Francisco. This physical manifestation of the Bitcoin network may help alleviate concerns that it exists "out there" and isn't rooted in any sort of real-world tangibility. This is to say nothing of the countless nodes being run by Bitcoiners around the world or the hundred of Bitcoin meetups taking place in cities from Seattle to Jakarta.

When you work hard and earn money, there is an underlying and innate expectation that the money you earn is actually yours. Money is meant (in part) to serve as a store of the value you've created in the real world. It is a representation of your time and effort. It is reasonable to expect that once an employer or a customer has paid you for your product or service, that money belongs to you to do what you want to do with it.

What if (and hear me out) your money was just yours and no one else's? What if when you earned a dollar, you could sleep at night knowing that this same dollar that you earned today, would offer the same purchasing power as it will in 20 years? I know that is a radical thought experiment, but if you really boil it down to first principles, common sense, and logic, that is simply how economics can and should work. Instead, we are forced to earn a dollar today that is worth 50 cents tomorrow due to monetary manipulation by factors outside of our control. We are forced to bankroll wars that we don't consent to and we are forced to risk our hard-earned money in casino-styled schemes like stocks, bonds, and mutual funds in order to tread water and keep up with inflation. This is important to grasp because we've been gaslit and conditioned to believe (and subsequently expect) this reality is normal.

Pay Me in Bitcoin

I'm teaching my kids about money by putting my sats where my mouth is. It's not enough to just teach your offspring about modern economics and to simply earn, save, spend, and give. You cannot criticize the fiat monetary system within your family without bringing forth a superior solution. One of the best parts about putting this habit into practice is watching how your kids begin to truly value self-sovereignty and strive to earn and save more. Thanks to Bitcoin's unique properties, it also helps them experience money in a way that pre-Bitcoin generations could only dream of experiencing.

My kids have come to prefer being paid in bitcoin because they've watched both their personal wallet's value and their satoshi spending power increase since they started earning it from an early age. Saxyn even said recently, "I wish I had stacked more when I was younger!" (a common sentiment once you learn about what makes Bitcoin unique). The discipline of saving has become underrated in our fiat-infested world because we intuit that our money is melting. If we don't spend it as soon as we earn it, we've already learned that it will not go as far in the future. Spare your kids from having to get caught up in this infuriating form of brainwashing by helping them learn how to preserve their little egg nest in their own self-custodied wallet that they alone control. Teach your children to demand to be paid in Bitcoin because they value the time, effort, and contribution they expended in order to earn those precious sats.

THANK GOD FOR BITCOIN

The best way to understand Bitcoin is to first understand the current monetary system and ask the question that my friend Robert Breedlove has popularized: What is money? In my last co-authored book *Thank God for Bitcoin*, we explore the moral aspects of our current economic reality and compare that to the opposite dynamics represented in Bitcoin. I would encourage you to check it out if you're looking to learn more about the non-technical reasons Bitcoin has resonated with so many of us. I've had the opportunity to take my kids to multiple Bitcoin conferences and Kingston has earned the rank of co-organizer at our local Bitcoin meetup and landed internships at Bitcoin companies.. Being around other Bitcoiners in real life is one of the fastest ways to get to the bottom of what's going on with this magic internet money. When you get to know the people behind the protocol, you can't help but notice a common thread of critical thinkers who for some reason or another got tired of playing the game of life with monopoly money. They called BS and decided to opt-out of the rigged game upon realizing they could not win. Instead, they opted into a truly sound monetary network that is backed by proof-of-work and cannot be manipulated.

When you work your whole life within a system that continually robs you of the fruits of your labor, it is easy to become weary, cynical, and bitter. But once you discover Bitcoin, you are renewed with a sense of hope that a better way is possible and is unfolding among this community of humble and energized trailblazers. This sense of renewed hope and optimism for the future is a much better frame of mind to adopt for every parent. My family and I are citizens of the expansive, diverse, and revolutionary community of Bitcoiners. Our kids earn, save, and spend in satoshis. Their future is more secure than ever, not because of my 401k, but because of their self-expressed quest for sovereignty. Once you experience these truths and it clicks for you for the first time, don't be surprised if you find yourself saying, "Thank God for Bitcoin."

Section 3 Next Steps

- Evaluate the presence of screens in your home, including how often you are personally on a device. Write down a realistic plan to establish a set number of hours for screens for your family. Set parental controls if available. Make a distinction between content categories (educational, entertainment, etc.) and allocate time accordingly.

- Call a family meeting. Establish a clear and firm "No Screens at the Table" rule effective immediately. If necessary, confess your own personal struggle with this in the past and your commitment to the new rule moving forward. Enforce this new rule at every meal, both at home and while dining out.

- Consider the tasks and responsibilities around your home that would make for instructive, paid roles your kids could take on. Have fun with the process by making it as close to a real-world hiring and onboarding process as you can. Set up an interview with your kids, create a written offer letter, schedule a training session, and establish paydays (bonus points for paying them in bitcoin).

SECTION 4
Can You Hear Me Now?

We now turn our attention to one of the most common struggles parents face: getting their kids to simply listen to them. This is not an easy topic, and we'll tackle it from multiple angles throughout these chapters, which are largely dedicated to discipline. Sound Parenting asserts that it begins with mindful and CLEAR communication and a callback to utilizing precise language.

If the word "responsibility" is my all-time favorite word in the English language (as discussed in Chapter 4), a close second is the word "clarity" and its nephew "clear." We've already seen this demonstrated with the mantra "Clear over Cute." There's additional evidence in one of my go-to phrases: "Clarity Is Reasonable." We'll explore one final aspect of this robust word, unpacking the exciting and never-controversial topic of discipline and its correlate of obedience.

Obedience is one of those words that makes many people uncomfortable. You've probably guessed that I'm not one of those people. When tweeting about a few of the keys you'll find in this section, the pushback from strangers on the internet suggests that the potential for this section to be a bit spicy is high. We'll look at some discipline mantras and methods Danielle and I have employed in our parenting since the kids were very young, including a foundational insistence that "Delayed Obedience Is Disobedience."

As a bit of a disclaimer, this section contains practical strategies for discipline that are most applicable to parents with younger children. There's no specific age limit to determine how helpful these tips might be, but as with many parenting tactics, often the younger the child is when they're applied, the more effective they will be in producing fruit. While these steps are not for the faint of heart, they do become easier if they are carried out with intentionality as part of a broader parenting strategy.

CHAPTER 14
BE CLEAR

A ll the way back in Section 1, we discussed the lost art of simply talking to your children. Parental habits which form the basis for how communication will take place between parent and child begin forming at a very young age. In fact, we acknowledge that in many ways we begin setting the tone for how we interact with our children with the snowballing effect of every prior interaction from their inception until the present moment. We observe this dynamic in pregnant mothers who sing and talk to their unborn baby. We sense that infants recognize the voice of their father which sounds oddly familiar and consistent with a voice they heard for the past nine months. Your children not only know your voice, they also intuitively understand you are the default authority in their life. This begs the question: why won't they just listen to what you say? In other words, why won't they *obey* me?

This is a critical question to explore, and I believe it is helpful to genuinely wrestle with the answers that emerge when it's given proper consideration. It's usually "asked" as more of a rhetorical question or an exasperated cry for help like "he just won't listen!" But the question *can* be answered and strategies must be implemented to foster healthier communication with your child which can lead to greater obedience.

There are five aspects of developing a Sound Parenting family culture and the imperative of obeying Mom and Dad. These can be easily remembered with another handy dandy acronym CLEAR:

Calm Communication
Loving Commands
Enforcement Consistency
Appropriate Consequences
Repetition Constantly.

Let's break these down one by one.

CALM COMMUNICATION AND LOVING COMMANDS

If you are yelling or raising your voice, chances are you've already lost the battle. If you are overly emotional and cannot deliver your instruction with a CLEAR head and balanced temperament, there's a good chance it will fall on deaf, defiant ears. You must be calm. You are the adult. Chances are the situation may be frustrating, but it's unlikely to warrant you losing your cool. You cannot expect your little human to gain control of their emotions if their parents fail to do so. This is perhaps the most obvious of the five steps, but it is still worth mentioning that Sound Parenting requires approaching every interaction with emotional maturity. We're not looking for fear-based parenting. Your delivery is everything. It's not only a matter of ensuring your child isn't terrified of your instruction, but also remaining calm ensures that the words you are using are intentional.

At the same time respect is earned. In order to arrive at a place where your children more easily obey your instruction, it is essential to ensure that you are delivering loving commands and choosing your words carefully. What is the intention behind what you are communicating? Is it logical? Is it in the child's best interest? Or is it selfish to your immediate needs and plainly an abuse of power? Kids will see right through a hollow demand for obedience and understandably revolt against a parent with a power trip. In some ways, if the parent is self-aware, this can be encouraging. This again is where introspection allows you to discover the answers to your own questions. Perhaps they are not listening to you because your commands are egregious, inappropriate, or plainly unloving. If that sounds harsh, I'd point you back to Chapter 6 with a gentle reminder that I'm not saying you are those adjectives, but that from time to time, we as parents would do well to remember that we are not perfect and our emotions can get the best of us. I know I've had such moments of unreasonableness where if I'm being honest, I wouldn't have listened to me either.

ENFORCEMENT CONSISTENCY AND APPROPRIATE CONSEQUENCES

I cannot stress this enough. **If you are not consistent with your approach to discipline, you will fail before you even**

start. Write that one down. This means communicating clear boundaries and the consequences for breaching those boundaries BEFORE they are violated. Kids, like adults, need consistent expectations. They do not like surprises any more than you do, especially when it is disruptive to their sense of peace. When you speed on the highway, you know that you are liable to get pulled over and receive a ticket. There is no shock when a police officer pulls you over for doing 87 in a 60 and issues you a ticket for $275. That is the law. You might not like it and wish you got off with just a warning, but at the end of the day the punishment fits the crime. You were fully aware that you were opening yourself up for this exact outcome by speeding. The same level of enforcement consistency must be true for your kids as well.

Not only do you need to be consistent in enforcement, but you also need to ensure that you've clearly outlined appropriate consequences in accordance with the nature of the offense. Overly excessive consequences are just as ineffective as soft, inadequate consequences. It is important to establish parameters based on your child's behavior. If you have a child who is prone to lying, you must clearly communicate what happens next time they lie. The same is true of hitting, disobeying, not sharing, whining, and so on. Each category of undesirable behavior must be met with a predictable and appropriate consequence. It must be communicated frequently and well understood in the household. Ideally, you can gain agreement with your children about what appropriate consequences look like. Call a family meeting and have that conversation today. Get their input. Ask them what they think is reasonable. This works for almost all post-verbal ages. We've been holding family meetings since our offspring could walk and talk, explaining that if they perform X behavior, then they will receive Y consequences. By doing this well in advance of having to enforce said consequence, there is much less resistance. If you are successful in establishing these boundaries outside the emotional context of an infraction taking place, you will have much more success delivering the consequence than you otherwise would when everyone is emotionally invested in the heat of the moment. Delivering random consequences on the fly is almost always a failing strategy.

REPETITION CONSTANTLY

To round out the CLEAR acronym, it's critical to emphasize the importance of repetition. Part of the goal is to evoke automatic responses to the point where your child is finishing your sentences. Make your own mantras. Make them portable, sticky, and easy to remember. Then repeat them. Often. You may get the occasional eye roll and you will even annoy yourself from time to time. But if you are intentional with your parenting plan and truly believe in the methods you've laid out, you can be confident that what you are conveying is valuable to your desired end goals as a loving parent. From there, repeating yourself becomes necessary and automatic.

CLARITY IS REASONABLE

I want to call to mind this book's title the next time you're wrestling with the persistent need to enforce your own household rules. It's a way to level set and not only reclaim your authority, but also reaffirm your profound responsibility. "I am not your bruh" communicates clearly that you are the parent. Your child needs you to continually shepherd them with loving, thoughtful, CLEAR instruction, even when they are wailing or attempting to negotiate.

Several years back I founded a non-profit organization whose mission was focused on demanding that pastors be clear regarding their church's actively enforced policies. We didn't attempt to convince pastors to change their stances or revise their policies, but rather insisted on them being explicit in disclosing them to avoid people being misled. To effectively convey the reasoning behind our mission, I coined the tagline "Clarity is Reasonable," which I believe is a widely applicable phrase and a relevant reminder in a parenting context as well. If you are going to assert any level of authority, it is in fact *reasonable* to expect the scope of this power to be clearly defined. If you are unable to articulate your policies, rules, and the consequences for potential infractions, it is difficult to expect those impacted by your authority to properly abide by these ambiguous mandates. Further, it is completely *unreasonable* to lack clarity regarding your expectations and then enforce unpredictable consequences when those unspoken rules are violated.

Being CLEAR is not something that happens by accident. It requires time, thoughtfulness, and a willingness to be proactive. It takes effort to develop a cohesive parenting strategy and it requires energy to see it through. These tools can offer some basic frameworks, but the heavy lifting is found in the individual parenting plan you create that is most appropriate for your household. The key is to actually have a plan and ensure you stick to it.

CHAPTER 15
THE TROUBLE WITH "TROUBLE"

Parenting is more art than science. It is a constant balancing act that requires frequent calibration based on changing circumstances. As a parent, you are changing at the same time your children are changing and the world is changing. Change is the only real constant. But while the dynamics of parenting can be unpredictable, there are several core truths and foundational habits that can serve as pillars for parents. As mentioned earlier, this starts with vocabulary. Language is extremely powerful. **With your words as a parent you can cultivate safety, develop trust, and create joy. You also have the power to evoke fear, sow suspicion, and cause sadness.** The words we use don't just result in binary outcomes like "good" or "bad" but can also result in more complex outcomes like confusion or curiosity. At the end of the day, we are planting seeds in the lives of these little humans. And with parenting, you do in fact reap what you sow, perhaps more acutely than in other areas of life.

In the Mekhail household, we have a handful of words and phrases that we actively avoid and sometimes openly mock (even with our children). When describing a scenario where our kids have made a poor decision, we do not tell them, "You are in trouble." Likewise, when they make a mistake and come to us and ask, "Am I in trouble?" we respond with "No" because of our obsession with precise language. "You're in big trouble!" is a meaningless, unhelpful, fear-evoking phrase that is counterproductive to our actual desired outcome. This is where the requirement of being more mature than your children and rising to the occasion of Sound Parenting comes into play. It's not enough to get frustrated and shoot off at the mouth all the ways in which your child fell short of your expectations. Venting, lashing out, and even intimidating your offspring may be cathartic in the moment, but is it really cultivating the type of human you want to eventually send out into the world? Of course not. By resorting to an overly emotional reaction and firing off phrases about how much "trouble" they are in, you are only serving yourself and attempting to alleviate your own pain and disappointment. You are also most likely rejecting the uncomfortable truth that this "mistake" your child has made is far too reflective of the brand of mistake you are accustomed to seeing in yourself and your own patterns of behavior. Yikes! Who's really in "trouble"?

The point is, when you habitually say, "You're in big trouble, mister!" you're not actually saying anything of value. Parents often recite these types of phrases because they are stunned and maybe feel helpless in response to the unexpected or defiant action of their child. Do you really mean "Wait 'til your dad gets home" or, in reality, are you just delaying corrective action and avoiding remedial conversation? The word and ambiguous concept of "trouble" is simply creating additional anxiety and unnecessary confusion.

THE THREE A'S

When your child makes a mistake or a poor decision, your responsibility as a parent can be broken down into three necessary steps for a complete resolution, though in practice, they may not always follow this order:

ADMISSION: Help them understand and acknowledge their error by clearly outlining how they fell short and guiding them to arrive at this conclusion as well. Depending on the severity of the offense, this can be firm but doesn't need to be ominous or threatening.

AWARENESS: Give them space to talk through what happened, why they did what they did, and what they wish they would have done differently. This is where asking questions and expressing empathy can be most powerful.

ACTION: Delivering a corrective response by articulating the real-world consequences of their actions and, if possible, gaining agreement that this is the appropriate response considering what they admitted to and their awareness of what they did.

Don't hate me, but I'm going to invoke the golden rule again: "Do unto others as you would have them do unto you." For some reason, our default as parents can tend to exclude our own children from eligibility as "others." But the reality is quite different: We have a responsibility to develop their own understanding of their divine right to be treated with dignity, respect, and understanding. Now that doesn't mean they are our peers or friends by any stretch, as the title of the book suggests. Rather, it means parents have an obligation to teach and cultivate this sense of individual personhood in their child.

Often this starts with reflecting back to the child the very simple reality of the way in which they fell short. Let's explore a simple example scenario step by step:

Admission

"Did you slap your baby brother in the face?"

"No..."

"Are you sure? Because he's crying, he has a red hand mark on his cheek and he's pointing at you."

"No, I didn't do anything!"

"Are you telling the truth? Because the only thing worse than slapping your brother would be lying about it, so please take a moment and think about your answer."

"Ok fine, I slapped him, but I didn't mean to."

The reason this step is important is because you can imagine how tempting it would be to simply jump the gun with accusations, a verdict, and sentencing. The evidence is clear. The defendant is obviously guilty, and there are seemingly 21 million more urgent priorities to tend to than presiding over a trial when the facts are so plain. However, these are the moments that require parents to slow down and actively... parent. **The quick and easy path is rarely the one that produces the best fruit.** In this scenario, immediately jumping to the defense of the crying child can be quite consequential. I'm convinced that young children are the most observant of all humans. They notice everything. Quickly defending the crying child without question will communicate to both children that mere accusations are sufficient for determining one's guilt in nearly every situation. Not to get overly cute with the legal analogies, but in many ways skipping "due process" can easily spiral out of control in future scenarios. The crying child can become manipulative if they are subtly taught that the parent will defend them simply by producing a few tears. More importantly, by leveling accusations prematurely, you can rob the offending child of the opportunity to confess, come clean, and most importantly own their error.

Admitting to one's shortcomings is a critical habit to cultivate in the early stages of human development. If we go through this life with the attitude that we are always innocent until someone accuses us of wronging them, we will be a very difficult person to deal with and struggle in almost every relationship. We will rarely take responsibility for our actions and prioritize pushing the boundaries of what we can get away with in almost every situation. At the same time, if we grow up in an environment where we are prematurely accused of things we didn't do and made to feel like we are always "in trouble," we are more likely to turn out defiant, defensive, and despondent. Admission is the healthiest possible outcome for everyone in the scenario.

Awareness

Every situation is obviously going to come with multiple, complicated variables. The age of the child, the frequency of the habit in question, the severity of the offense, and so on.

But the rubric for guiding them through these situations can remain consistent. After the confession comes awareness, which is the immediate response when genuinely realizing an offense has been committed. If this step is overlooked, especially in younger children, you will likely have a quick, inauthentic confession followed up by a disingenuous "sorry" and desperate desire to quickly move on. Anyone can say, "Ok fine! I did it! I'm sorry, okay!?"

This doesn't result in meaningful change or healthy habit formation. There can be no self-reflection or demonstration of remorse without true confession. This step is accomplished by intentionally cultivating awareness (a contender for my 3rd favorite word). Here is a possible follow-up to our brother slapping scenario:

> *"Thank you for telling the truth. You hit him, but you didn't mean to make him cry. What did you mean to do?"*

Notice the power of questions and the importance of emphasizing language. As mentioned previously, we must not let our kids get away with lazy words and empty language. If you say it, mean it. And say it with your whole entire being: none of this word salad, empty platitude, used car salesman garbage phrases. "I didn't mean to" is often as meaningless as, "You're in trouble" or "I don't know." By calmly and matter-of-factly asking simple questions, we can uncover the most fascinating conversations and sometimes even turn difficult situations into unexpected teaching moments. Challenging your children to respond to simple questions is an incredibly effective method of teaching accountability. "Why did you slap your brother? What did you mean to do? Would you want someone to slap you? Do you like it when your brother slaps you?" These are very basic and potent inquiries that often go unasked by parents. This step requires the most patience and can take time. But time is your ally. Believe it or not, you have access to more patience than your child in these situations. They can only stand the discomfort, awkwardness, and embarrassment for so long. **Deep down their guilt and the innate sense of shame when they commit a real offense acts as nature's teacher. You are simply a steward of what is already going on within them.** Wait it out. Ask more questions. Don't let it go until you are satisfied with their eventual demonstration of true awareness of the situation.

> *"I guess when I think about it, the reason I hit him was because I wanted him to jump rope with me, but he didn't want to jump rope. That made me mad, so I hit him."*

Boom. The jump rope bandit has nowhere to turn. Internal screams of, "What have I done!?" now begin to consume the assailant. The child is now confronted with the difficult reality of their own self-realized error. There is nowhere to turn but inward. Good! As a parent, you have so far managed to navigate potentially treacherous terrain. You are not the source of some unjust punishment or the bringer of false accusations. The child has arrived at their own conclusion, and they recognize that they are the only one to blame for the tears, questions, and the looming consequences. The defendant has pleaded guilty. Next comes the most difficult and necessary step: action.

Action

The category of discipline is wide-ranging. One facet that seems to be on the minds of many parents is the controversial disciplinary tactic of spanking. Should you spank your kids?

Answer: no one knows. Personally, we spanked Kingston a handful of times when he was very young, still running amuck in diapers. We were also very young and likely a little immature. When defiance occurred, we sat him down and calmly explained the situation and why a spanking was being issued. We were adamant not to hand out spankings willy-nilly or in anger. At times it seemed effective, and at other times it seemed to create even more defiance. Sometimes it seemed justified and occasionally it seemed like we were reacting too emotionally. By the time Saxyn was born we started to feel less and less like spanking was the right choice. Maybe because she's a girl and he's a boy? Maybe because she's younger? Maybe because she has a different temperament? Hard to say. Parenting is dynamic. Some kids probably do benefit from a light swat on the bum from a genuinely loving and intentional parent. For other kids, this is likely the worst thing you can do to achieve your desired parenting goals. It's not so black and white.

There are entire books dedicated to the subject of parental discipline from spanking to grounding and everything in between. I believe that discipline is a skill to be taught, meaning it's less of a verb as in, "What do you think about disciplining your kids?" and more of an attitude as in, "I aspire to teach my kids to be disciplined."

That said, I am not a proponent of punishment: another subtle but important vocabulary distinction. Punishment is typically used in the context of enforcing a penalty or retribution for a wrong. Parents need not be punitive when correcting their children's shortcomings. Instead, the most effective method of delivering corrective action is to simply allow for clear, consistent, and natural consequences.

In the scenario described earlier, the clear, consistent, and natural consequences depend on what precedent has been established in your home. There are several ways to go about this, but the key is properly categorizing the offense and carrying out the appropriate action that the child is already expecting. It cannot be random or unreasonable. With enough practice, the child will even anticipate the consequence immediately after awareness sets in.

Danielle and I may seem intense in our parenting, and we're okay with that perception. We believe that shielding kids from the fact that they will face real-world consequences in their life is not doing them any favors in the long run. Let me illustrate this point and the action stage simultaneously with a story from Kingston's childhood. When he was about four years old, there was a short stretch of time where for some reason getting him to put his shoes on for school became a persistent struggle. One day, we decided to simply allow him to go to school shoeless. At first, after his surprise subsided as he considered what his day would be like with no shoes, I imagine he felt as though he scored a major victory in the great shoe rebellion by getting his way. But the predictable Seattle rain made sure this was the last time we had to ask him more than once to put on his shoes. On this fateful day we removed any doubt as to our willingness to let him "win" and allow nature to (quite literally in this case) deliver the lesson that our words were otherwise failing to convey. Truth be told, there were no winners in this situation. We obviously didn't want him to go to school shoeless any more than he wanted to experience soggy feet. But the valuable lesson after the fact was ultimately worth one day of discomfort and inconvenience for us and for him. When words and reasonable instruction fail to produce results, action is your only recourse as a parent.

The tone of our debrief conversation after school that day was less intense than you might imagine. At that point, walking him through the other two As was a piece of cake. It was rather easy at that point for him to *admit* where he fell short and become *aware* of the impact of his disobedience while reflecting on the obvious decision to avoid this *action* in the future.

There is no substitute for allowing children to experience an immediate cause and effect of their actions when appropriate. Again, the key is consistency in enforcement. Following through on each of the As regardless of how the situation unfolds is essential to ensuring the lesson is properly learned and minimizes the chances of the same offense reoccurring in the future. While the three As include the need to deliver a sincere and meaningful apology, we place even more emphasis on what happens after the fact for maximum effectiveness. I like to say, "The only authentic apology is changed behavior," which means, "The proof of sincerity will rarely be realized immediately after the words 'I'm sorry' are uttered."

All that said, the real goal of parenting is attempting to avoid these situations as much as possible by teaching your children that often what's in their best interest is to simply listen to your loving instructions the first time you ask.

CHAPTER 16
DELAYED OBEDIENCE IS DISOBEDIENCE

⊶

We're all familiar with the scene. A child throwing a tantrum in a public place while their helpless parent is pleading, almost begging them to knock it off. As the classic standoff escalates, the embarrassed parent is left with no choice but to reach into their tool belt and attempt to take control of the situation. What is the most common tool employed in this situation? The countdown method of course:

1... 2... don't let me get to 3... 2 and a half... Aubrey, you know what happens if I get to 3, no more iPad... ok that's it, 3!

What happens next is usually very anticlimactic. The tantrum rarely stops and the embarrassment is now uncomfortably felt by onlookers in the form of pity and judgmental eye rolls. Worst case, the empty threat of removing the iPad becomes the very thing that is used to attempt to quell further escalation. The power struggle is real, but utilizing the "countdown to consequences" tactic is almost always counterproductive. It works against the parents' end goal and is subtly teaching the child that they have at least three more prolonged seconds to act up before their parent's instruction might actually mean anything. If you are still utilizing this method, I want to first implore you to stop. It doesn't work. The countdown always fails and you come out on the other end weaker than where you started. Next, I want to encourage you to adopt a different mindset: Delayed Obedience is Disobedience.

COSTCO CHAOS

There are few things more dreadful than a trip to Costco on a Saturday. After stalking numerous shoppers throughout the parking lot, identifying a person who might be leaving, then throwing your blinker on to lay claim to your prize, you get to wait patiently as they unload their overflowing cart of groceries. Parking is half the battle, but when you have a toddler, as was the case for Danielle shopping with Saxyn one fateful weekend, the fun was only just beginning. After successfully retrieving all the items from her list and proceeding to the checkout line, Danielle was feeling like she was about to escape unscathed. That's when Saxyn decided she needed Goldfish crackers. When the request was gently denied, "no sweetie, we already have Goldfish crackers at home" a meltdown ensued. At Costco. On a Saturday. At the checkout line.

Danielle paints a picture of Saxyn pulling out all the stops, determined to get her way. We're talking top-of-the-lungs screaming, theatrics which ranged from the classic jumping up and down to flailing uncontrollably on the floor. Refusing to panic or show any sign of giving in, Danielle remained calm, ignored the tantrum, while stepping over her child and proceeding to greet the cashier and wrap up the transaction. By not acknowledging the active manifestation of "the terrible twos" playing out at her feet, she was subjected to the condemnation of onlookers, silently questioning her judgment and parental acumen. Unphased yet uncomfortable, Danielle confidently proceeded toward the exit, receipt in hand prepared for the highlighter checkpoint. You won't believe what happens next: after realizing that her mom was not playing games, and briefly experiencing the separation of only a handful of feet, Saxyn surrendered her fight for the Goldfish crackers, jumped up off the Costco floor, and ran to Danielle's side, quiet as a mouse. No countdown, no empty threats, just unwavering commitment to the principle that delayed obedience is disobedience.

Of course, Danielle never intended to actually leave her at Costco to fend for herself, and even as she began to walk away kept her comfortably within her line of sight. Additionally, she had a keen awareness of Saxyn's temperament and foresaw the effectiveness of her selected strategy (in other words, don't try this without ensuring you know your child will respond in kind). It's also important to note that there's nothing particularly unusual about Saxyn's request or reaction to being denied Goldfish crackers. There's nothing surprising about a child making demands and expecting them to be met. It's like being shocked at an infant crying when they are hungry. This is all part of early development. No child is automatically obedient and expecting them to be only leads to frustration. In order to unlock this coveted behavioral milestone, parents must be fully present to their child in all the ways we've discussed.

The "Five More Minutes" Myth

We've all been there. It's bedtime, and your child is deep in play, constructing the most magnificent LEGO castle or lost in the magical world of a fairy tale. The mere mention of "time for bed" is met with the age-old plea, "Five more minutes, please!" Seems harmless, right? What's another 5 minutes? LEGOs are good for fostering creativity, you reason with yourself, while granting the wish. However, we know what happens next: 5 minutes turns into 15, another plea to get ready for bed is met with another request for an extension. And why not? It worked the first time. The minutes can quickly turn into hours, and what starts as gentle pleading turns into angry shouting, frustration, and lashing out. Similar to the dynamics at play with the doomed countdown method, many parents fall into the 'five more minutes' trap, falsely seeing it as a way to ease the transition. But in reality making these 'small' compromises sends a hidden message that your words are flexible and negotiable. The child begins to understand that they can stretch those five minutes into an eternity, rendering your instructions ineffective.

It is essential to realize that every time you give in to the 'five more minutes' request, you're inadvertently teaching your child that your initial instruction was ignorable. Consistency is key, and it's vital to ensure that when you set a boundary it remains unwavering. It won't be easy, especially when faced with those puppy dog eyes and earnest pleas. But by demonstrating consistency and adhering to your own boundaries, you're teaching your child the importance of respect, discipline, and a timely response to instructions. This may sound harsh ("Oh come on, it's just some extra LEGO time, George, live a little!"). But, it's precisely these 'small' compromises accumulated over years of adolescence that later begin to manifest in much more serious and undesirable traits.

So what's a parent to do? Go in there, kick the LEGO structure down, and let the kid know you mean business? Obviously not. In order to actualize the mantra that "delayed obedience is disobedience," specific tactics are needed. It doesn't happen overnight, but with enough practice, patience, and precision, you too can avoid the dreaded bedtime negotiations.

YES, DAD. YES, MOM.

I will admit that this rule of thumb requires significant practice, commitment, and consistency before it is well understood by young children. It requires you as a parent to initially embrace your authority and potentially suffer through the awkwardness of public tantrums without giving in or resorting to the more humiliating knee-jerk response of counting down. That said, by implementing somewhat unconventional tactics, you can begin to cultivate the appropriate response to your instruction. The goal is to convey that anything less than immediate obedience to your commands is unacceptable.

I want to address the underlying controversy that emerges anytime I speak of "obedience." First, it is important to clarify that I'm strictly speaking to *parental* authority. This isn't meant to convey, by any stretch, that automatic obedience to ALL authority is the goal. We're talking about Sound Parenting. I'm not your boss, I'm not your teacher, and I'm not a police officer. I'm your father. It is also important to note that cultivating habits of obedience and respect for Mom and Dad's authority is most effective in young children. Once they are past the toddler years, this method can quickly become overbearing and devolve into knee-jerk utilization of one of the worst phrases any parent can ever utter: "Because I told you so."

That said, we trained our kids early in their lives that there are exactly two appropriate responses to our instructions:

Yes, Dad.
Yes, Mom.

That's it. There is no wiggle room or modifications here. This is the level of clarity and appropriate boundary setting that young children ultimately crave. Remember, young kids literally have no other frame of reference for their decision-making besides what their parents teach them. So, if appropriate response mechanisms are not proactively taught, children will seek outside influences and their own selfish desires to guide their decision-making. The same is true if they are passively taught that it is acceptable to delay parental obedience or if they observe inconsistencies in how their parents enforce instructions. "Yes, Dad," ends the discussion. This is not a negotiation. We are not doing bribes or issuing empty threats. We are undertaking the holy work of bringing up mature and responsible human beings who honor and respect the people who brought them into this world and who love them more than life itself. End of story.

CHAPTER 17
OBEY FIRST, THEN ASK QUESTIONS

In the previous chapter we established that "Delayed Obedience Is Disobedience" and outlined the reasons for insisting young children listen and obey parental authority from the jump. We now turn to a related mantra: "Obey First, Then Ask Questions," which offers parents a simple, straightforward retort anytime a command is challenged. At first blush, this may sound overly dismissive or synonymous with the dreaded "Because I said so." However, we must consider the statement as a whole in order to fully appreciate what is being proposed.

As we've explored, a critical aspect of Sound Parenting is to move from theory and good ideas to pragmatic solutions that are simple to implement. Parents looking to establish authority, increase dialogue, and encourage critical thinking must be clear communicators first and foremost, especially when it comes to discipline and correction. When a phrase is repeated with clarity and consistency, a child begins to not only memorize your words but the subsequent seriousness of your actions. The forcing function we are encouraging here is to eventually arrive at a place where the mantra is rarely needed; the child simply obeys and responds with "Yes, Dad" or "Yes, Mom" and if they have questions, they know they will have the opportunity to ask, only after they have followed your instruction.

Safety First

When we are talking about instilling the need for obedience in young children, I've learned that it is essential to establish this baseline respect for the seriousness of parental authority from an early age if you hope to influence your children in a healthy and positive direction. Not only that, heeding your commands promptly can sometimes become a matter of a child's safety and well-being. Young children can often be aloof and in their own world. This is understandable as their imagination is beginning to expand and their desire to explore becomes unbounded. You might even need to yell "STOP" in a moment of sheer panic as they are running around outside, unaware that they are wandering near a street. In these split-second moments, it becomes clear why the seriousness of your voice and urgency of your instruction must be heeded the first time you ask. I know it's not fun to explore such extreme hypothetical scenarios, but the thought experiment is not far-fetched and hopefully drives home the importance of my point. The same is true for less-intense situations, even if the consequences may be milder.

"Obey first" is a firm, non-negotiable command which delivers a level of unwavering instruction designed to quickly and matter-of-factly assert authority. This is especially effective for establishing authority with very young children when they first begin to challenge your instructions. **But I must emphasize that the statement is not complete without ensuring you communicate and give room for "Then Ask Questions."**

It is important to address sensitivity around the idea of obedience to alleviate potential concerns about parents abusing their power or stifling genuine curiosity and critical thinking in their children. That is far from the goal and why encouraging questions about your instruction is an essential part of the formula. "Obey first" is simply a more portable conveyance of "Delayed Obedience is Disobedience"—whereas "Then Ask Questions" is the mechanism for follow-up teaching.

For example: imagine you're at your in-laws house, picking up your kids from a sleepover at Grandma's. After packing the car, visiting with your mother-in-law, even finishing a cup of tea or whatever, you are finally ready to head home, and by the look on her face, Grandma is also ready to have her empty nest back. Here's how a hypothetical scenario might play out:

Ok, Jefferson, time to get your shoes on and say good-bye to Grandma.
But whyyyy I'm still playing. I don't want to go!
Jefferson, obey first, then ask questions.
Yes, Dad.
Thank you. We can talk about it in the car.

Young Jefferson's resistance was short-lived, and good for him. Admittedly, this scenario would likely only be this smooth after some consistent practice from the parent, and perhaps a Costco story or two under your belt. But assuming you make it to this stage, let's unpack the critical second half of our mantra—"Then Ask Questions?"—by picking up the scenario on the drive home from Grandma's house:

> *Jefferson, I know you were having fun at Grandma's and it was time to leave before you were finished playing. Do you have any questions about why it was time to go?*

Here, we're acknowledging that playtime was disrupted and inviting the child to gain a better understanding of what might have felt like an abrupt and perhaps even seemingly "unfair" demand. Often there are no questions, but ensuring they have a chance to inquire helps foster a level of trust for your instruction.

> *Why did we have to leave? Grandma has the best toys.*

> *Yeah, I love how much you enjoy playing at Grandma's. It was time to leave because we don't want to be late picking up your sister from piano lessons.*

While this example isn't particularly dramatic, it is still helpful for young Jefferson to understand why it was time to leave Grandma's, even if the answer is not super interesting. Critically, by insisting on obedience first, you eliminate real-time bickering, whining, and negotiating, even if the reasoning is simple. It is in these mundane follow-up conversations where taking the extra step as a parent demonstrates to your child that you are not just winging it or throwing around your authority without reason.

As any parent will attest, kids have a lot of questions. One thing I've noticed is parents can be lazy with the art of drawing out questions from their children in a way that effectively affirms their curiosity. This is especially true in situations where discipline was just carried out and emotions are still raw. These are often the best moments to encourage question asking: while it's fresh. The point is in the engagement with the question and validation that it's okay to ask. The best part about going out of your way to ensure your kids ask questions is how much the floodgates tend to open into completely unrelated yet productive topics of conversation. These are priceless and sometimes formative moments that deliver some of the best gifts of the entire parenting experience.

Benevolent Dictatorship

Your home is not a democracy. When you are raising young children, you are not seeking consensus in your parental decision-making. Most things are non-negotiable. Don't let this get to your head, but Mom and Dad are the final decision-makers in any healthy home. This posture may sound "authoritarian" and will be intentionally misunderstood by critics who are uncomfortable with any form of healthy leadership. The truth is, some parents are afraid to lead because modern society has become soft and skeptical on the matter. As a result of our quest for increased "inclusion" in all things, I believe we have relinquished any semblance of healthy, effective, and necessary leadership across many domains of our world. This includes the workplace, government, and reverberates all the way to the home front. The pendulum has swung too far in the direction of my generation's unfortunate and misguided paradigm that everyone is a winner. Millennials are known for being "trophy kids" for a reason. We've been led to believe that autonomy should be granted the minute a baby emerges from the womb. I call bullshit.

Young kids need their parents to be firm, unwavering, and confident in their demeanor. Anything less fosters a deep level of insecurity in the child, which ultimately leads to rebellion and disrespect. Bedtime is not up for negotiation. "Don't eat the Play-Doh," isn't a mere suggestion. Following simple rules established within the household by loving parents is the path to order. Remember when we had rules? Crazy idea, I know. There was also a time when winning zero games and finishing dead last on a soccer team meant you did not receive a trophy. However, this was not my experience. I still remember the pizza party "celebration" and last place trophy I received when I was ten playing on a soccer team that literally didn't win a single game all season. It is no wonder my generation is uncomfortable with this topic. Autonomy is a rite of passage, embraced by children as they learn how to fend for themselves. By attempting to relinquish authority too early in the name of "equity" or whatever other buzzword we're striving for, we're saddling children with an undue burden of responsibility prematurely.

Recall from the previous chapter that kids are very observant. I believe kids are far more perceptive than most adults give them credit for. In fact, they are so perceptive that they understand this very simple dynamic I'm describing: parents should lead and children should follow. Children have the ability to sniff out weakness and sense danger if they are not being adequately guided. Why do you think they mock the countdown method so confidently? The goal isn't to stifle your children with unnecessary commands just because you can. I'm assuming the reader is more mature than that. The goal is to assert a loving, caring and benevolent level of authority that is consistent with your natural desire to see your children flourish. This isn't an invitation to go on a power trip. This is a reminder that your children not only need boundaries, but they desire the comfort of your guidance.

CHAPTER 18
WHINERS GET NOTHING

I imagine many parents with toddlers read the previous chapters with heavy doses of skepticism or disbelief. "So, your kids just obey you all the time and say 'Yes, Dad' to whatever you ask?" Answer: it took some time and they are not perfect, but for the most part, yes. They quickly learned to respect and trust the authority and instruction of Mom and Dad to the point where we rarely need to ask more than once. They often took us up on the "Ask questions" part, and this cadence has produced some of the healthiest conversations of their upbringing. We did not arrive there by accident, and any parent can achieve the same results with a similar level of intentionality.

We know that parenting is exhausting on a few different levels. When your kids are younger, the majority of the strain is physical. For moms, this fact is obvious in pregnancy, childbirth, and the weeks that follow delivery. From there, the physical toll continues rather intensely with a long period of sleep deprivation, which impacts their body in every other aspect of their days. This is to say nothing of the simple, yet compounding efforts required to pick up a child, rock them, play with them, pick them up again, change diapers, maybe throw them in the air, buckle them into the car seat, push them in the stroller, take the car seat out, put the stroller in the car, pack their bag, clean up vomit, fiddle with the car seat some more, etc. You get the picture. As your kids grow, the work involved in being a parent begins to shift from mostly physical labor to a spike in mental and emotional labor. The acceleration of this dynamic happens around the time they begin forming sentences and becoming aware of their individual personhood. With this critical realization comes increased demands for their needs to be met, and the various and unsavory forms in which they choose to assert these demands.

SHOW ME YOUR INCENTIVES

One of my favorite things about Bitcoin is its near perfectly designed incentive structure. Miners are required to take the risk of expending valuable energy resources for the hope of successfully finding a block and earning the block reward. Holders of bitcoin are incentivized to run a node to contribute to greater distribution (or decentralization, if you prefer) of the network, further protecting the viability of their asset. Incentives are powerful motivators of human action and children are no exception to this innate feature of being alive. Learning about human incentives and becoming more mindful of how they work and what makes people tick has been one of the most valuable lessons I've learned from being a Bitcoiner and has served me in powerful ways as a parent.

A positive incentive is naturally meant to elicit a desired behavior. Salespeople are trained to understand that the main question a prospective client is asking boils down to "What's in it for me?" before they make a purchase. An effective salesperson focuses on answering this question to close a deal. The inverse of creating positive incentives to induce the desired behavior is ensuring clear disincentives are present for undesirable behavior. When the kids were very young, a frequently repeated mantra in our home was, "Whiners Get NOTHING!" We established very early on that whining would not be tolerated, mostly because it's annoying but also because it points to a deeper sense of entitlement that needs to be nipped in the bud.

Fact: no one likes a whiner. Most of the time, whining is tied to some sort of request. Often sugar is involved. Regardless, the key here is to make it absolutely clear that the correct way to make a request does not involve a whiny attitude, because whiners get nothing. This mantra is meant to shut down the unsavory behavior without a hint of consideration for the request in question. Every parent would agree that they don't want whiny kids, yet the reason it's worth specifically addressing is to encourage vigilance in this area as a key aspect of Sound Parenting.

Don't Be a Victim

Closely tied to this key is the reminder that victimhood can sometimes be subtly championed (if not celebrated) in our present culture. These days it can seem appealing to seek ways to identify as a victim, which can often begin with finding something to be offended about. Ultimately, this apparent shortcut to gaining sympathy or preferential treatment is not a healthy mindset to adopt, even if the short-term incentives suggest otherwise. This one is a bit more touchy because there are of course actual victims who have experienced incredible pain, injustice and heart ache in their lives. I don't discount the real-world circumstances of those who have endured unthinkable trauma, often no fault of their own. But even in those unfortunate scenarios, some of the most inspiring stories of restoration tend to emerge. In other words, people who are *actual* victims, who have faced seemingly impossible circumstances, often find a way to forge ahead and reclaim their life and their story by essentially declaring, "I am not a victim." They refuse to wear that label, even though they have every right to submit to the accuracy of the descriptor. The point is that even if being a victim in some situations may be justified, it is not a helpful posture or mindset to adopt.

Disclaimers of actual victimhood aside, feigned victimhood seems to be more common and is among the least attractive habits one can possess. Children who are permitted to feel like the cards are constantly stacked against them or that such and such "isn't fair" are conditioning their brains to identify as a victim. The concept of fairness itself is overrated and overused. I'm not suggesting utilizing the phrase "life isn't fair," which while accurate isn't always helpful. The responsibility of parents when it comes to addressing creeping victimhood requires much more effort than pithy phrases. It's incumbent on the parent to redirect these attitudes in a way that encourages resilience rather than resignation. This means encouraging kids to lean into struggles and hardships instead of giving up when faced with life's many challenges. It means helping them show up even when they don't necessarily feel like it. It means watching self-talk and practicing self-awareness. It means not tolerating constant complaining while offering support and coaching to pursue realistic solutions to even minor problems.

One very practical tip on this point is for parents with toddlers. When Kingston was learning how to walk, I remember how often he'd fall down and immediately start crying. At first, we would rush to offer our doting and comfort, but after a while, we realized that he would sometimes milk this behavior for attention. We had subtly taught him that if he fell down and started crying, he'd almost immediately get picked up by one of us, which is frequently a top priority for a toddler struggling to take their first steps. We'd been duped! Once we caught on to his fake falls, we changed our behavior and instructed grandparents and babysitters to do the same. "You're okay" is the phrase we used moving forward, followed by patient endurance of the subsequent wailing. He had to adopt a new strategy, and low and behold, not too long after that he learned to walk on his own. We continued utilizing the phrase "you're okay" as a helpful tool for similar situations when our kids actually fell down for real or expressed some type of discomfort or pain. The knee-jerk temptation from a loving parent is a strong reaction anytime their kids are (seemingly) hurting. This is of course natural, and in extreme cases obviously necessary and warranted. But if an audible gasp and quick intervention follows every minor cry for help or every small expression of pain, kids can drift into an early onset understanding of the surface-level incentives to adopting a victimhood mentality.

Solutions Oriented

We are raising children who Use Their Words and have the ability to lean into their vocabulary in order to communicate a request. It takes time to develop this skill, especially with young children, but by being unwavering when it comes to not responding or giving in to whining, you can begin to guide your children to articulate their request properly. This includes using manners and as they get older understanding the types of requests that are appropriate for a given situation (i.e., self-awareness). Sound Parenting requires intentional coaching when it comes to helping children lean into critical thinking to become problem solvers. You cannot solve every problem for your kids, and resisting the urge to save the day can be the hardest habit to learn, especially for new parents.

Depending on the age of the child and the nature of the request, sometimes they can be whining over a problem that they have the ability to resolve completely on their own. Other times they are making a request that needs to be denied for one reason or another, but in an effort to appeal the decision resort to whining in an attempt to get their way. In either case, the role of the parent is to first shut down and not entertain the whining, and then help them understand a more appropriate path to make their request as well as the conditions under which the request would be considered and eventually granted. One helpful tip for navigating these situations is to replace "no" with "not right now" if the situation allows. Follow it up with clarification on when the request might be granted, as long as the child is not whining. This is closely connected to "obey first, then ask questions," but is distinct in that we're identifying a slippery slope to a poor character trait which parents must be proactive in eliminating as early as possible.

Being solutions oriented is another important habit that impacts several areas of life and is essential to learn at an early age. While the initial response of "whiners get nothing" seems harsh, the intention is to plant seeds that foster greater self-reliance, critical thinking, and ultimately problem solving. By demonstrating that whining is not the path to get what you want in life, you're training your kids to seek alternative methods of making requests and solving whatever problem they are facing. Sometimes the solution is recognizing that a particular request is unreasonable and not asking is the appropriate course of action.

Whining is one of those things that can be sneaky in the ways it manifests and creeps in. It can be a simple result of lacking the skills to express an emotion or a desire. Or it can be a habit that's picked up by kids, like many things, by simply observing and parroting their parents. If you find yourself with an overly whiny child, consider reflecting on how frequently phrases like "I'm so tired" or "I'm so bored" or "the weather sucks" or "I hate my job" or "this TV show is so annoying" are expressed in your home. When we are lazy with our own words, we can't expect our children to make a distinction as to what is appropriate for them to note as acceptable. We set the tone, and if we are frequently setting a whiny, complaint-ridden tone, we are communicating that these forms of expression are acceptable in our children. The greatest irony within this common dynamic is when parents complain about their kids in general (let alone complain about how much their kids whine). If you find yourself doing this, and your underlying desire is wanting to have kids who are less whiny, the reminder I want to offer is the same for adults as it is for kids: Whiners get NOTHING.

Section 4 Next Steps

- Set aside some time to write out a comprehensive discipline plan. Craft it according to the age of your children and their unique temperaments, struggles, and personalities. If you are married or co-parenting, make sure you develop this plan with your spouse or additional parents and gain agreement on every aspect.
- Call a family meeting. Discuss the differences between real-world consequences and "punishment." Share your plan, but present it as a "draft" so that you can include your kids in some of the particulars. Communicate that the parents will have final say, but that you also want their input.
- Establish the "Whiners Get Nothing" mantra in your home. Repeat it often and encourage your kids to finish the sentence "Whiners get..." when appropriate.

SECTION 5
Family Business

We all have a story. Collectively, you and the other members of your household are writing a shared story. Every family has their own mantras, house rules, and traditions that are interwoven with each other while constantly evolving into a unique mosaic. Our role as parents requires us to remain mindful and intentional as our kids begin to write the initial chapters of their own individual story without being overbearing with every stroke of the proverbial pen (or MacBook key). Every day and every parenting decision we make plays a role in how their story is shaped, for better or worse. Many of these topics are somewhat personal in nature, and that is perfectly acceptable. A level of privacy is healthy and even necessary within the family unit. Not every moment in your home, whether positive or negative, requires a social media post. In other words, this is Family Business.

In this closing section, we touch on aspects of spirituality, dive deeper into character development, and zoom out to examine proper expectations for parents. Determining how you will approach these consequential topics ultimately becomes the rubric for defining your success in your quest to become a more effective parent. The setup to these themes begins with some self-reflection on our own mortality and the encouragement to Number Your Days. By forming habits of examining the fragility of our lives, we become better equipped to guide our children by prioritizing the Sound Parenting imperative of proper character development.

Regardless of how you might describe your own spiritual journey, whether you pray, go to church, or read the Bible or other sacred text, there are fundamental truths which are universally applicable to all of humankind. We'll unpack the ancient wisdom contained in the biblical "Fruit of the Spirit" and how keeping these simple, common sense traits top of mind can serve as behavioral signposts which are critical to emphasize as we go about the work of raising our children. Finally, we conclude with a critical reminder about remaining realistic with your expectations and graceful with yourself and your kids every step of the way.

CHAPTER 19
NUMBER YOUR DAYS

⚷

I have this random, arbitrary goal of living until I'm at least 80. This is where the mantra of "No Regrets When You're 80" originated. The reason I've even set a goal to begin with stems from my reading of Psalm 90:12 which says:

So, teach us to number our days, that we may apply our hearts unto wisdom.

I realize that this passage doesn't exactly say, "Set a goal of how long you want to live." I also realize that unlike a weight loss goal or a goal to quit an unsavory habit, you can't exactly control how long you're going to live. But for me and my type A personality, giving myself a target date for a potential expiration of my life provides a concrete way to number my days in the event I happen to reach my goal. And if I don't, well, I'm dead, so it doesn't matter anyway. There are 29,220 days in 80 years. That means, at 38 years old, I have a maximum of about 15,340 days left. When you really break it down like this, you begin to more acutely realize that each of our precious lives are extremely limited, even if we make it all the way to 80. Every human eventually reaches the same fate, and we all learn that time is the final boss.

The question then becomes, what have I done with the 13,879 days I've already lived and what will I do with whatever time I have left? This is a sobering level of self-reflection if we take the exercise seriously. But in practicing to number our days and teaching our kids to do likewise, we can unlock even greater levels of intentionality with each day we are blessed to be alive. Every day is a gift. Life is fragile. We are each one split-second decision away from years of regret, extreme consequences, and irreversible troubles at any given moment. To truly know where you are going, it's usually helpful to start by considering where you've come from.

Beginning on your own, consider the following exercise: open a new spreadsheet and name it "Life Timeline." Title the header columns Year, Age, Grade, Major Events, Residence, School, Job, Teacher, Church, Main Influences, and Stories. Fill in the "Year" column starting with the year of your conception all the way to the current year. Then start filling in the rest of the cells with the corresponding information. Feel free to add other columns that are appropriate to your own unique journey. For instance, multiple jobs you've held at the same time, various business ventures you want to document or hobbies you had at various intervals, etc. The point is to make it yours and take the time to reflect on your life at a very basic but detailed level. At first glance it might seem that there is nothing extraordinary about writing down such simple facts, like which house you were living in way back in 2004. But I believe that by going through this process and then continuing the habit of numbering your days in this way, you will grow in self-awareness and begin to cherish each day just a little more. You will also begin to recall periods of your life that you haven't thought about in a while and maybe even see how some of those moments, teachers, or neighborhoods had an impact on where you are today. Imagine how powerful such a simple tool can be for a young child whose life is just getting started.

WRESTLING WITH GOD?

You may have noticed that I've mentioned faith and spirituality and even used some biblical principles throughout this book. My goal in doing so is not to try to convince you to believe the same things that I believe about God. But the reality is every parent must wrestle with what to teach their kids about this hot topic, regardless of where you personally land.

Everyone has a "God" story. Whether you're a Christian, Muslim, Mormon, Buddhist, or even atheist, you have at one time or another had to confront the questions pertaining to God. For most of us, there is more than one question and we spend our entire lives continually revisiting each of them, changing our minds, then changing them again. More than likely, we continue to repeat this cycle throughout our days until the end. I believe our posture toward these questions and our attitude to that which is mysterious has a significant impact on our parenting.

As for me and my house, we've traveled across the spectrum of beliefs at some point or another and continue to approach topics about God and faith with curiosity and humility. A perfectly acceptable answer when it comes to the topic is "I don't know." You don't have to have it all figured out, and in fact, sometimes the people who claim to have it all figured out are among the worst representatives of their professed faith. I grew up in the ultra-conservative Coptic Orthodox Church, eventually left for a moderately conservative evangelical church, and then ended up working for a mainstream evangelical church which over time became increasingly progressive. Danielle grew up Baptist, followed by evangelical, and then our paths merged as we were both asking similar questions about what we believe. Throughout this journey, we did our best to bring our kids along. **Rather than insisting they embrace dogmatic religious claims, we've focused on teaching our children how to approach the exploration of faith**. To summarize a few truths that I would consider essential:

- All humans originated from somewhere, presumably the same place, mysteriously.
- Whatever or whoever brought us here did so out of a similar type of motivation as aspiring parents who want to bring life into the world.
- If your notion of faith doesn't create imitable character qualities, your faith is worthless.

Almost every other truth claim is basically secondary.

INDOCTRINATION IS NOT CUTE

As I mentioned earlier, Danielle and I both grew up in Christian homes. Finding a Christian spouse was a prerequisite for both of us and our faith was a foundational aspect of our early dating and married lives together. Within a couple of months of our relationship getting serious, we realized that the Foursquare church I had been attending was MY church and it was very difficult to integrate her into a community that I shared so much history with long before I met her. We decided to find a church that we could call OURS, which led us to a new startup church called EastLake. This would become a formative decision and the place we'd spend the next ten years of our lives helping build. In 2009, I left my career as a banker to join the staff at EastLake as their Executive Pastor. Life started coming at us quickly from this point on. Within a few years both Kingston and Saxyn were born, while the church was growing exponentially. This also meant my kids spent a good portion of their early childhood with a pastor dad. In the biz, we call such kids "PKs" or Pastors' Kids.

We read to our kids from the *Jesus Storybook Bible* every night before they went to bed. We prayed with them and tried to instill Christian values as best we could. However, we were also cautious about *forcing* a Christian worldview on them if there was resistance. We both had plenty of that from Danielle's Baptist and my Coptic upbringings. To this day, this is the posture we take when it comes to teaching our kids about the Divine. We offer our individual perspective, we answer their questions, but we never force faith on them. I'm thankful that we had the wherewithal to allow them to discover their faith without the pressure of needing to live up to our expectations or believe the things we believe in order to earn our love or support. This is the biggest mistake I see parents making when it comes to the touchy and at times controversial topic of what to teach your kids about God, religion, and faith. Indoctrination isn't cute and it can rob your children of their individuality. Not only that, but it can often work against your desired goal and end up creating kids who never genuinely embarked on their own spiritual journey. This typically ends with a shallow, fabricated faith built on the convictions of the parents, rather than an authentic process of discovery led by the child.

This is not a simple topic and there are more questions than answers. But regardless of where you land, even if you're atheist or agnostic, my encouragement is to tread lightly when it comes to creating expectations, fear, or demands for your kids around their spiritual path. Obviously, share your faith. Obviously, if you attend church, take them with you. If you feel compelled to pray or read the Bible with them, do that. But qualify your convictions as YOUR convictions and leave some breathing room for them to come to their own conclusions. Do not suffocate them with your anxieties or make them feel like a sinner every time they step out of line.

Believe it or not, it's not your job to resolve this universal tension for your children, and trying to force a belief on anyone, especially your kids, is a fool's errand. Do more showing than telling. It's not impressive to simply say you believe in God or attend church. What's impressive is exhibiting admirable qualities which creates curiosity in your kids about what makes you the way that you are. At the end of every numbered day, the goal of Sound Parenting is to prepare kids for the real world by providing the tools for them to become people of high character. Ultimately, what determines whether you're finding success in this consequential aspect of parenting is as simple as observing the fruit that is being produced in your life and the lives of your children.

CHAPTER 20
FRUIT OF THE SPIRIT

⊢

As I've mentioned several times, our north star in parenting is character development. It comes up in just about every corrective conversation and every coaching opportunity we have with the kids. We often ask, "Who are you becoming?" and yes, we lean into some core truths from the Bible that serve as benchmarks for answering this question. Galatians 5 says:

> *But the Fruit of the Spirit is love, joy, peace, patience, kindness, goodness, faithfulness, gentleness, self-control....*

People who exhibit these behaviors are people you want to be around. Children who are taught to produce this fruit are children who are being trained to possess sound character qualities that become foundational as they navigate the ups and downs of life. These interconnected traits help form the basis of healthy relationships and build the foundation for sound decision-making, and it's worth taking a closer look at them to understand their particular value to parenting.

Kindness, Gentleness, and Peace

We've already spent the better part of a chapter discussing kindness, so I'll be brief. Within the context of a Fruit of the Spirit worth emulating, kindness is the simple trait of thinking about others and actively exercising the golden rule. It's as simple as that. Treat other people the way you would want them to treat you. That's what it means to be kind. To truly live into this habit requires a proactive posture, seeking out opportunities to extend kindness and cultivate a heart of generosity toward loved ones. In the same way you wish others would do unto you, extend kindness and teach your kids to do likewise.

I've been encouraging a level of assertiveness as a core aspect of Sound Parenting—speaking up, using your words, not avoiding confrontation, etc. To be truly effective when carrying out these tactics, a degree of gentleness is appropriate. This is consistent with No Name-Calling and Limiting Absolutes. Being overly harsh, dismissive, or unreasonable is not the goal when dealing with others, including in our everyday approach to parenting. For instance, when you are correcting your children, you will find that carrying a poised, level-headed, and gentle tone is the most effective approach to communicate your expectations and lead them to the outcome you're seeking. This is once again a fruit that is best modeled through your lived example as much as it is important to verbalize the goal of cultivating gentleness in your kids.

It's not controversial to suggest that our world has a bit of a peace deficiency. There's not a lot of peace going around these days. People who possess this character quality are natural problem solvers. They see an issue and they go to work to find a solution. Rather than exasperate, complain, or escalate an issue, people of peace attempt to find common ground, lean into logic and reasoning, and ultimately deliver harmony where there is chaos. Counterintuitively, this skill requires the ability to thrive under pressure and learn to become comfortable with confrontation. Peace must be actively pursued. Aspire to cultivate a peaceful home which is warm and inviting. Teach your kids to develop habits of sowing peace where there is chaos and show them how with the example that you set in your interactions and problem-solving abilities.

Patience, Faithfulness, and Self-Control

One of the most obvious and self-explanatory fruits of the spirit is the quality of patience. If you have young children, your patience will constantly be tested. As your kids become teens, hopefully you've gained some practice in this area, because you're going to need it. One qualifier regarding patience is to practice discernment in situations where you've been sufficiently patient or are being asked to be more patient than what is reasonable. We're not raising doormats here, and sometimes in life if you are *too* passive in the name of patience it can be easy to get taken advantage of. Perhaps you've earned your keep and that promotion is long overdue, or maybe you've waited for that boyfriend to put a ring on it for long enough and he's needlessly dragging his feet. These situations may not call for more patience, and acting assertively to adequately address these types of scenarios does not necessarily mean you do not possess this fruit. The true mark of patience is perhaps more recognizable by its opposite quality of impatience. The key is to recognize when a situation calls for patience and having the ability to exercise it when appropriate. Patience is also closely linked with forgiveness. This means that you can move on from situations when you were hurt in a healthy way and with adequate resolution without being bitter or holding a grudge. I believe that when you implement some of the keys we've been discussing, you will create opportunities for your kids to become more patient.

Being faithful is a quality of people with integrity. A true mark of faithfulness goes beyond the obvious categories of things like marital faithfulness or not cheating on a test. Faithfulness also boils down to everyday habits such as doing what you say you're going to do with consistency, being reliable, and ultimately dependable. No one likes a flaky person. As a simple example, in the Mekhail household we emphasize the importance of being on time and expect our kids to be punctual as a matter of respect for other people's time. This is such a critical aspect of high character people and glossing over the need to develop everyday faithfulness is a recipe for losing respect, developing a poor reputation, and in extreme cases becoming untrustworthy. Once you go too far down this road, it can be difficult to recover. Be faithful in all your endeavors and demonstrate for your children that your words are consistently connected to your actions.

Self-control is perhaps one of the most important (if not most underrated) parts of the fruit of the spirit. Everything we've been discussing requires the habitual practice of self-control to achieve any level of success. People who are overly impulsive or who frequently act purely from emotion often end up making decisions they regret. This isn't to say

that feelings or emotions are bad, but simply to acknowledge that they can have an outsized influence in our knee-jerk
decision-making. The key is to help your kids navigate these
heightened states of emotion, which is easier said than done.
Developing self-control is one of the most difficult challenges
that we are presented with in life. It's strange to think about
how hard it can be to get our own self under control. We
frequently do things we don't want to do, eat things we know
we shouldn't eat, or procrastinate or neglect things we know
we need to get done. Focusing on this trait alone can exponentially impact your satisfaction with your everyday life. Training
your kids to practice self-control makes every other key that
much easier to master. Once you decide who you want to be
and what you want to do with your life, which is made up of
the days you've begun numbering, the next step is to align
your actions with those outcomes.

Joy, Love, and Goodness

One of the foundations of American ideals is "the pursuit of
happiness." This is a worthy aspiration, and as a 1st generation immigrant, I believe America delivers on the promise
to provide the *opportunity* for everyone to pursue this goal.
But while they are interrelated, happiness and joy are not
the same thing. For instance, someone can chase "happiness" and still end up being lonely, depressed, or dissatisfied.
You can be happy on the surface while deep down still long-
ing for true meaning. Joy instead comes with a deep sense
of contentment and satisfaction with life. It is a delicious
and delicate fruit that is marked by a person's energy and

excitement for simply being alive. People who effectively "show up" exude a level of enviable joy that is contagious. Being joyful means being undeterred by setbacks, failures, and missed expectations.

We all know what love is and why it's important. You love your kids, otherwise you wouldn't be reading this book. The concept of love can be nebulous and difficult to nail down, it's almost one of those things that humans intuit more clearly than we can otherwise describe verbally. It is of course essential to demonstrate genuine love with our actions. This is especially true in our posture toward our children, who have an astute ability to sense whether authentic love is being conveyed. At the same time, communicating the three magic words verbally is also incredibly powerful. We say "I love you" a lot in our home. Someone is leaving, someone is going to bed, hanging up a phone call, whatever—it's how we end an interaction within our family.

Love may be an overused word in general and the way we tend to use it in everyday language might cheapen it a little in some ways. I love my kids differently than I love a good steak— same word but different levels of impact and meaning. But when my kids remind me that they love me before leaving a room, even if we've had a rough day, my heart is assured that they are on solid ground and maybe, just maybe, I'm doing something right in their eyes. It's not often that we end an interaction without an "I love you" and "I love you too," but in the rare case this happens, it serves as a bit of a yellow flag that something might be off. I wouldn't recommend neglecting this simple habit. Constantly remind your loved ones that you love them. Don't be shy. Use your words.

The final fruit, goodness, is a bit tricky. It requires discrimination to determine what is considered goodness and what is considered badness. In our world, the word "discrimination" has become taboo due to it being tied to all the various "isms" that we're not allowed to talk about. But when I say discrimination in this context I'm simply encouraging the use of sound judgment. The quality of goodness is closely linked to kindness in that it is recognized by a person's unwillingness to participate in harmful behavior. To name a few, this means not lying, stealing, killing, or gossiping. But the list is much longer and requires individuals to judge for themselves. It's worth noting that while most humans can agree on some of the main attributes of goodness, there are clearly going to be other examples where what you define as "good" your neighbor may define as "not so good." This only further demonstrates the need for parents to proactively and intentionally define for their own household how they will approach this topic and how they will train their kids in the ways of goodness. For starters, I would suggest not approaching this one in a vacuum but having it exist within the framework of the broader set of parenting keys we're discussing throughout this book.

Teaching your kids these traits is not about making sure they are Christian or following the Bible. This is once again just taking ancient wisdom at face value and acknowledging there is deep truth contained in the idea of exhibiting these qualities. If we hope to raise kids who prioritize long-lasting, highly impactful attributes that make up their character, it is helpful to speak directly to these nine simple descriptors and allow them to serve as guideposts along the way. I'm not impressed when people tell me they are spiritual, religious, or that they believe in God. What I am impressed by is when people consistently demonstrate love, joy, peace, patience, kindness, goodness, faithfulness, gentleness and self-control. Some people may have a hard time with this positioning, and as a former pastor I want you to know I understand where you're coming from. I want to be clear that I'm specifically being critical of any faith, belief system, or parenting strategy that fails to produce the type of humans who exhibit these qualities. Even Jesus himself said, "You will know them by their fruit."

CHAPTER 21
PERFECTION IS NOT THE GOAL

Parenting isn't rocket science. It's much harder. With all due respect to all the rocket scientists out there, the implications of a failed launch are far less consequential than the implications of a failed parenting strategy. One of the main purposes of writing this book is to encourage parents to become aware of the importance of their role while developing and implementing a cohesive strategy that produces results. While I hope I've offered some practical steps that have worked in my own home, the truth is most of the keys we've discussed are straightforward and somewhat basic. I was reviewing my Kindle library and was a little surprised to find 12 different parenting books Danielle and I have read throughout the years (and many more if you count physical books). Different authors have found and will continue to find different ways to say 80% of what I've said throughout these pages. While some of my acronyms, mantras, and tactics have elements of originality, I'm under no delusion that I'm the first person to offer similar anecdotes for effective parenting. What it really comes down to is what will be memorable and applicable enough for readers to put into practice. Again, this is hard work. The steps might be relatively simple, but that does not mean results will come easy. To once again recall a principle from Bitcoin: the results we see reflected in our own kids are an outcome of proof-of-work.

Deciding to adopt one or many of the Sound Parenting keys is up to you, and I believe if you are motivated to take me up on some of these steps, you WILL struggle in the beginning and encounter several roadblocks along the way. But if you stick to it, eventually you will begin to see results. It's a lot like working out: you're not going to lose 10 pounds after a couple workouts. You must remain committed, consistent, and patient with your efforts in order to produce the outcome you are seeking. Most people can't just show up to the gym and start randomly doing exercises without a clear goal and a plan for which exercises to do, how much weight to lift, and how many reps to perform.

In the context of parenting, this translates into doing the initial work of intentionally developing your own parenting plan and making the conscious decision to stick to it. You're not going to sporadically fall into better parenting habits if you don't set aside time to identify which keys you consider valuable, adding your own unique flavor, and seeing things through with your spouse or people in your life who spend meaningful hours with your children. The first step is taking control of your parenting, which requires you to create an actual strategy. Write it down. Draw a picture. Create a PowerPoint presentation. Whatever you need to do to formalize the steps you're committing to carrying out and hold yourself and your family accountable to real-world execution.

Is That a Plank in Your Eye?

The wide-ranging dynamics of parenting require us to acknowledge that every child is unique, every age is different, and every environment has distinct challenges. Unlike working out or rocket science, there will be times when even a clearly defined plan will require adjustments, improvisation, and your innate parenting wisdom. As long as you're striving to improve yourself as a person and putting in the work of becoming the best parent you know you can be, it's perfectly okay to allow for real-time dynamics to reveal new lessons along the way. Even by choosing to read this book, you've taken a measurable step toward meaningful improvements. I believe your kids will one day thank you for accepting the call of investing in their development beyond simply providing for their basic needs.

One of the main themes we've explored throughout this book has been the importance of working on yourself as a person in an effort to become a better parent. It is in many ways the piece of the puzzle that connects everything else together. I realized this one evening as I was getting ready to hunker down and write with a deadline fast approaching. Kingston was showing me a new video game he was playing and before leaving his room, I reminded him that he needed to clean up his room because it was a mess. Immediately upon walking into my office, I was confronted with my own hypocrisy. I don't want to say it was messier than my teenage son's room, but let's just say the motivation to sit down and write about parenting quickly gave way to a sudden urge to remove the plank in my own eye and bust out the vacuum. On one hand, I was a bit embarrassed and later made this confession to Kingston. He laughed it off and commended my self-awareness in an ironic moment of the student becoming the teacher. On the other hand, as I was furiously tidying up my office, I was inspired by the simplicity and power that comes from holding myself to a higher standard. Ensuring my office is clean is no revolutionary act, but in doing so, my authority to give this instruction to my child becomes exponentially more effective.

The sage wisdom Jesus offers in the Gospels (Matthew 7:3-5) is applicable to parents:

> How can you say to your brother, "Let me take the speck out of your eye," when all the time there is a plank in your own eye? You hypocrite, first take the plank out of your own eye, and then you will see clearly to remove the speck from your brother's eye.

Despite the common usage of this verse as applicable only to adult relationships, if we simply replace the word "brother" with "child" you've got a solid TL;DR for a key theme of this book.

My Biggest Fear

I have wrestled with whether or not to write this book for some time. It requires a level of vulnerability to share our unfiltered approach to parenting, knowing that some of the tactics will be misheard, misunderstood, or misapplied, not to mention judged, jeered, and joked about. But at the end of the day, discovering and utilizing the tools in this book has been impactful to the point where it felt important (if not necessary) to put into words and share with whomever will hear it. I am clearly proud of my kids and believe my wife and I are doing our best to parent them. With that in mind, they are by no means perfect kids, and we are by no means perfect parents. I shared with Kingston and Saxyn as I have been working on this project that my biggest fear in writing a parenting book would be unintentionally creating a sense of pressure on them to live up to an unrealistic standard of perfection in order to somehow prove these principles "right." I found comfort in their response and it even helped me realize this chapter's key: Perfection Is Not the Goal.

Your kids are going to annoy you. Then they are going to frustrate you. Then they are going to disappoint you. Then 11 am will roll around and they will do it again 37 more times before the day is over. They are going to make decisions that you don't agree with. They are going to believe things that you don't believe. They are going to hang out with people you don't like. They are their own unique, individual human with their own personality and aspirations. Your job is to embrace the mess and do your best: it's about influence, not control, and progress, not perfection.

If we strive for perfection, we're doomed to fail before we even begin. You will never be 100% consistent with carrying out whatever parenting plan you decide to implement (even just now in that last sentence I used an absolute—see what I mean?). Sometimes our lofty expectations are the biggest blocker for making any improvement. Progress is a more attainable goal to strive for, and taking steps that lead to meaningful change in areas in which you're seeking change is all you can really hope for.

Parents who take their mandate seriously do so with fear and trembling. They recognize that even despite their efforts, they are not going to be able to predict every outcome. We are in the business of pain mitigation and character formation. These are among the least sexy job descriptions imaginable despite the job itself being the single most important job on the planet. If you've accepted the call and are eager to embark on the journey of Sound Parenting, congratulations—you're literally a leader in my book. And I don't know about you, but it sure seems like there is a leadership deficiency in our world. We need more people to step up and accept the call.

Parenting is the most challenging and most rewarding responsibility afforded to us in this life. Imagine bringing a whole entire human being into this world who is a literal piece of you and not being awed by such a profound blessing. What a gift! I invite you to increase your level of intentionality with each precious day you're entrusted with the honorific of "Mom" or "Dad." You will make mistakes and they might even rebel. But they will never stop being your kids, even when they grow up and have kids of their own. You might find success in your career, or excel in a variety of different talents, but if you commit to prioritizing the habits of Sound Parenting, you will soon discover that ultimately, your family is your biggest flex. And it starts with the decision to embrace your child as much more than a friend and assert the gentle reminder that "I am not your bruh."

Section 5 Next Steps

- Complete the exercise outlined in "Number Your Days." Duplicate the file, empty the cells, and have your family also complete the exercise. Set a calendar reminder for every six months for reflection and adding additional milestones as needed.
- Call a family meeting. Be intentional about sharing vulnerably about the existential questions of faith, religion, and spirituality that you have wrestled with in your life or are currently wrestling with. Invite your children to do the same and create an environment that encourages them to ask deep questions. Be okay with not having all the answers.
- Make a list of your personal habits, both positive and negative, which are frequently observed by your children. Try to think of at least three of each: habits you'd be proud to see them emulate and habits you'd like to eliminate. Add to the list three more aspirational habits that you'd like to develop after reading this book.

Acknowledgments

Woooo. That was fun! Before we get outta here, I want to give the biggest shout outs to my wife Danielle, my son Kingston, and my daughter Saxyn. Thank you for the critical role you each played in making this book a reality, especially patiently listening to me talk about it for so long! Danielle, thank you for the countless hours you invested editing, proofreading, and contributing to this project with stories, ideas, and fact checks. Inshallah many mothers can learn from the wisdom you've shared and the example you set as a parent. Saxyn, thank you for designing the perfect cover for this book! I'm thrilled that your creativity will be the first thing people see when they pick up a copy. Also thanks for the TikTok story, honestly pure gold. Kingston, thank you for the late-night jam sessions, whiteboarding different topics, and the helpful feedback you've provided throughout the writing process. Not to mention the way you SHOWED UP to multiple Bitcoin conferences and meetups that led me to people like Allen and Sydney encouraging me to write this book.

To my parents, Samir and Theresa, thank you for instilling in me strong values and helping form in me the character that inspired me to take parenting so seriously. I still remember when Dad told me that his goal was for me to exceed him as a man and how impactful that has been on my outlook.

Big thank you to Peter McCormack for writing a thoughtful and heartfelt foreword. Thank you to my editor Olson who delivered timely insight into the overall structure of this book's contents. To my publisher, Ellen, who has encouraged me as a writer every step of the way, along with Mike who has championed this book from the start. The entire Bitcoin Magazine Books team including Kayla, Ben, Lana, Joe, Spencer and Reece who make all the behind-the-scenes magic happen, down to the critical step of helping you find this book and placing it in your hands.

Shout out to the pastors and mentors I've learned from throughout my life at various stages including my uncle George, Pastor Bob Hasty, Ben Dixon and Mark Driscoll, Jeremy Johnson, and Dave Nelson. Mike Meeks whose fingerprints are no doubt present throughout these pages as lessons I picked up from one of his sermons. Ryan Meeks, our pastor since marriage through the kids' early childhood, and his wife Michelle, who both provided countless parenting lessons, recommended numerous books and modeled admirable relationships with their family.

Thank you to everyone who has taken the time to read this book with an open mind. If you found it helpful, consider telling a friend or maybe even gifting them a copy and check out iamnotyourbruh.com for more.

Very special thank you to the GOAT Satoshi Nakamoto. Musical cameos by Michael Jackson, Salt-N-Pepa, Ice Cube, Kanye West, Carly Simon, You, Taylor Swift, Kendrick Lamar, and Destiny's Child.

All Praise and Glory to the Most High.

—G.

About the Author

George Mekhail is the co-author of *Thank God for Bitcoin*, VP of Operations at *Bitcoin Magazine*, and co-organizer for the Arizona Bitcoin Network. With a rich background in leadership, ministry, and family dynamics, George brings a unique perspective to each of these areas, blending practical wisdom with thoughtful analysis. Above all, George Mekhail is a communicator who cares deeply about the growth and well-being of individuals and communities. His writings are a testament to his commitment to fostering understanding, empowerment, and connection in an ever-changing world.

www.ingramcontent.com/pod-product-compliance
Lightning Source LLC
Chambersburg PA
CBHW030249130626
46549CB00002B/458